Your Very Good Health

Rose Elliot became a cookery writer by accident. She was planning to take a history degree when she met and married her husband and became involved in cooking, entertaining and having babies. It was while looking after the latter that she began scribbling down her recipes. These led to her first book, *Simply Delicious*, which in turn brought requests for cookery demonstrations. It was the invention of new recipes which led to her second book, *Not Just a Load of Old Lentils*, and patient research into recipes using pulses resulted in *The Bean Book*.

As well as writing regularly in the leading vegetarian newspaper *The Vegetarian*, Rose Elliot broadcasts and appears on television. When she is not writing and testing recipes, she enjoys studying astrology – which she uses in counselling – and caravanning with her husband and three daughters.

Simply Delicious, *Not Just a Load of Old Lentils* and *The Bean Book* are all available from Fontana.

Also by Rose Elliot

SIMPLY DELICIOUS
NOT JUST A LOAD OF OLD LENTILS
THE BEAN BOOK

ROSE ELLIOT

Your Very Good Health

FONTANA PAPERBACKS

First published in Fontana 1981
Copyright © Rose Elliot 1981
Second Impression 1983

Filmset in Monophoto Times

Printed in Great Britain by
Richard Clay (The Chaucer Press) Ltd,
Bungay, Suffolk

Contents

Acknowledgements

I would like to thank all the people who have helped me in the writing of this book. Firstly, my parents, who awakened my interest in health at an early age (as a result of their reading *Your Daily Bread* by Doris Grant, now reissured as *Recipe for Survival*, Faber).

I would also like to acknowledge the influence of two excellent books: *The Right Way to Eat* by Miriam Polunin (Dent) and *Future Cook* by Colin Tudge (Mitchell Beazley).

Finally, I would like to express my love and gratitude to my husband and two elder daughters, and to my parents-in-law who helped to take care of my toddler while I was writing this book.

Preface

During the past few years a growing number of reports have linked diet and health. Some of them suggest that we can improve our health considerably by eating certain foods and avoiding others. If you want to be fit yourself, and if you care about the health of those you cook for, how seriously should you take such reports? Is it really worth making changes in your diet, and how practical are they?

These were some of the questions in my mind when I started writing this book. I wanted to consider the theories and then find ways of implementing those which seemed important.

I found the task both demanding and satisfying. It was demanding because some of the facts I discovered forced me to reconsider ideas and to re-think cookery techniques which I had previously taken for granted.

What was satisfying, however, was that so many of the recommendations which emerged were eminently sensible and practical. In the light of these findings I am convinced that anyone, even the most dedicated gourmet, could make some worthwhile improvements to their diet without feeling deprived.

Incidentally, although I am a vegetarian myself and the recipes in this book are vegetarian, I am not suggesting that you should become one too in order to improve your diet. However, as you will see from the book, the evidence does point to the need to eat less animal fat and more fibre. Since even lean meat contains fat and as fibre is only found in cereals, fruits and vegetables, eating less meat and more vegetarian dishes is one of the ways in which you can make your diet healthier.

So I hope you will find this book useful whether or not you're vegetarian; that you'll enjoy the recipes and that they will lead to 'your very good health'.

Note on Measurements

In this book I have taken 25 g as the equivalent for 1 oz in all the recipes, and kept to the standard conversion table below. These conversions, whilst not exact, are the easiest to work with when cooking and as long as you keep to either metric or imperial measurements when following a recipe (and don't switch from one to the other) you should find that all is well.

However, for greater accuracy, in the sections on diet in the early part of the book, and when giving the calorie value of recipes, I have taken the more exact equivalent of 28 g to 1 oz.

Throughout the book the tablespoons and teaspoons used are standard size, 15 ml and 5 ml respectively, and level unless otherwise stated.

METRIC/IMPERIAL EQUIVALENTS

Grams (g)	Ounces (oz)	Millilitres (ml)	Fluid ounces (fl oz)
25	1	25	1
40	1½	50	2
50	2	75	3
60	2½	125	4
75	3	150	5 (¼ pint)
100	4 } (¼ pound)	175	6
125	4	200	7
150	5	225	8
175	6	250	10 (½ pint)
200	7	275	10
225	8	300	11
250	9	350	12
275	10	375	13
300	11	400	15 (¾ pint)
350	12 (¾ pound)	425	16
375	13	450	16
400	14	475	17
425	15	500	18
450	16 (1 pound)	550	20 (1 pint)
475	17	575	20
500	18	850	(1½ pints)
700	22 (1½ pounds)	1000 (1 litre) 35	(1¾ pints)
1000 (1 kilo)	2–2¼ pounds	1·2 litres	(2 pints)

OVEN TEMPERATURES

Temperature	Centigrade (°C)	Fahrenheit (°F)	Gas Mark
	70	150	
	80	175	
	100	200	
very cool	110	225	$\frac{1}{4}$
	120	250	$\frac{1}{2}$
	140	275	1
cool	150	300	2
warm	160	325	3
moderate	180	350	4
fairly hot	190	375	5
	200	400	6
hot	220	425	7
	230	450	8
very hot	240	475	9
	260	500	9

Equivalents for North American Readers

INGREDIENTS

Aubergine	Eggplant
Beetroot	Beet
Bicarbonate of soda	Baking soda
Biscuits	Cookies
Black treacle	Molasses
Caster sugar	Fine sugar
Cornflour	Cornstarch
Courgette	Zucchini
Double cream	Heavy cream
Grill	Broiler
Hazel nuts	Filberts
Marmite	Savita
Marrow	Squash/very large zucchini
Single cream	Light cream
Spanish onion	Bermuda onion
Spring onion	Scallion

MEASUREMENTS

1 pint (20 fl oz/575 ml)	2¼ cups
25 g (1 oz) chopped nuts	2 tablespoons
25 g (1 oz) butter/margarine	2 tablespoons
25 g (1 oz) flour	2 tablespoons
25 g (1 oz) grated cheese	4 tablespoons
25 g (1 oz) caster sugar	2 tablespoons
450 g (1 lb) fresh breadcrumbs	8 cups
450 g (1 lb) large beans	3 cups
450 g (1 lb) small beans	2 cups
450 g (1 lb) cottage cheese/quark	2 cups
450 g (1 lb) grated whole nuts	4 cups
450 g (1 lb) macaroni	3 cups
450 g (1 lb) mashed potato	2 cups
450 g (1 lb) cooked/uncooked rice	2 cups
450 g (1 lb) semolina	2 cups
450 g (1 lb) wholewheat flour	4 cups

How Healthy are You?

How healthy are you? How healthy are we as a nation?

Statistics show that one in four men in Britain and the USA will get coronary heart disease; one in four men and one in five women will get cancer; and one in twelve men and one in fourteen women will be admitted to general hospital every year. In addition, millions of working hours will be lost every year through colds, digestive upsets and other minor illnesses. Besides this, every day there will be many people just managing to get by feeling off-colour and below par.

We tend to think of ill health as something that's unfortunate and very bad luck but unavoidable. Of course sometimes it is, but increasingly research is showing that many illnesses come about as a result of our life style.

Smoking, and its link with lung cancer and bronchial diseases, is perhaps the best known example of this, but recent research has shown an equally dramatic connection between the kind of food people eat and the kind of diseases they are likely to get. Such conditions as gallstones, varicose veins, heart disease, mature-onset diabetes and diverticulitis are now all thought to be related to diet.

Some of the most convincing evidence of this has come from following the progress of people who, though born into countries with a primitive life style, later moved away. At first it was thought that these people might have a kind of genetic immunity to such things as heart disease, diverticulitis and so on because instances were so rare in their homeland. However, once they moved into the cities or to more developed countries such as the United States they began to get these diseases as much as anyone else. Much careful study led to the discovery that it was their new 'western style' diet which was causing the changing pattern in health. Those who moved but continued to eat in their traditional way remained 'immune'.

This particular research has been backed by other studies in

1

a number of countries. The picture they give us of the kind of diet most likely to lead to health is surprisingly consistent. It is also very practical.

The aim of this book is first to look at what makes a healthy diet and then to see how healthy eating can be put into practice.

What Makes a Healthy Diet?

Although the diets studied in the research differed in a number of ways, the healthy ones invariably had one thing in common: they all contained a large percentage of fibre foods and were low in fat and sugar. Fibrous foods supplied about 80 per cent of the day's calories and of the remaining 20 per cent, 10 per cent came from protein and 10 per cent from fat.

How does this compare with a typical British or American diet? In these, fat takes up 42 per cent of the calories and sugar 22 per cent with the remaining 26 per cent split between protein foods and carbohydrates. As the carbohydrates are usually refined, the fibre content is low. Also, quite a number of the foods in the British/American diet will contain some additional chemicals to preserve, colour or flavour them.

So there is quite a difference between the two diets, although had I been writing this at the beginning of last century there would not have been. Many people believe that 'we're eating the foods we've always eaten so they must be good', but this is not so. At the beginning of last century we were eating virtually no sugar and only 10 per cent of our daily calories came from fat. Since then our diet has gradually changed and as the consumption of fibre has dropped so that of sugar and fat has increased.

During this period medical records show that the incidence of many diseases has also increased. These include appendicitis, diverticulitis, gallstones, migraine, stomach and duodenal ulcers, angina, high blood pressure, heart disease and severe obesity.

Our diet is richer and sweeter today but not, it would appear, healthier.

Why should this be so? What's so wonderful about fibre and are sugar and fat really bad? How do saturated and unsaturated fats, fit into the picture – and what about cholesterol? And are food additives a cause for concern? Let's look at the issues more closely.

3

Fibre – What is it and Why is it Important?

Fibre is the name given to the structural part of fruits, vegetables and cereals. It's the cellulose, woods and gums which hold them together. We don't digest this fibre and it doesn't give us any nourishment, which is one of the reasons why it has taken so long for its importance to be recognized. Nevertheless fibre has a vital part to play in keeping the body healthy.

The presence of fibre in foods acts as a kind of natural rationing system. Fibre has to be chewed, and as there is a limit to the amount of chewing anyone can do, it prevents us from eating too much of anything. You might say this is nature's way of keeping us slim and, indeed, people on 'primitive' diets containing a high proportion of fibre don't get fat.

But the role of fibre doesn't end there. Just as we had to bite our way through the fibre to eat the food, so our digestive juices have to fight their way through the fibre in order to find all the goodness mixed up with it. This means that our body can cope with the nutrients gradually as they're drawn out and the whole process is methodical and systematic.

As the fibre travels along the digestive tract it absorbs liquid and becomes bulky, like a sponge. This means that the muscles of the intestine can get a good grip and move its contents along smoothly, quickly and efficiently.

If you take the fibre out of food you remove these natural safeguards. Sugar is perhaps the ultimate example of this. In its natural state sugar is found in fruits and vegetables and in particular in sugar cane and sugar beet, a tough root. If it wasn't for modern refining methods it would be impossible to eat more than a sprinkling of sugar even if you chewed all day long. As it is, it's easy to eat a bar of chocolate or several biscuits and hardly notice it.

So instead of the digestive system having to work its way slowly through the fibre to ease the goodness out, with refined foods this natural regulator has gone and the nutrients get into the bloodstream quickly, in a flood. The body has to take emergency action, releasing a great deal of insulin to digest the sugar. Whilst this may be all right occasionally, there is growing evidence to suggest that repeatedly straining the body in this way can upset the delicate mechanism which controls the flow of insulin, resulting in diabetes. (This is not yet fully proven but the facts are pointing strongly in that direction.)

Finally, of course, lack of fibre means that when the food passes through the digestive tract there is nothing to hold the water and provide the sponge like action.

Without the soft, water-holding properties of fibre, waste matter is dry and hard and more difficult to move along the intestine. It tends to break up and get stuck in pockets along the way. This is one of the chief causes of diverticular disease from which one in three people over the age of sixty suffer in the affluent countries.

Hard, dry waste matter also takes longer to pass through the bowel. This can lead to constipation and some experts think that, because the passage through the bowel is slow, poisons may be reabsorbed by the body and that this may be linked with the increase in cancer of the bowel in the industrialized countries.

The more you look at fibre, the more it seems to be fundamental to a healthy diet. So which are the fibre foods and how can you be sure you're getting enough of them?

FOODS RICH IN FIBRE

Recognizing the fibre foods can be confusing at first because the presence of fibre is not necessarily related to the texture of foods in the mouth. For instance, meat and fish are 'chewy' and appear fibrous but do not contain fibre, while banana and potato, which are smooth, do. Remember that dietary fibre is a vegetable product and is only present in cereals, fruits and vegetables such as:

Whole cereals – whole wheat, oatmeal and brown rice and products made from them such as wholewheat bread;
Bran, which is of course the fibrous part of whole wheat, extracted during the milling of white flour;

Dried peas, beans (including baked beans) and *lentils*;
All fruits and vegetables. The fibre in carrot and apple has been found to be particularly valuable because of its capacity to absorb water.

There is also a good deal of fibre in seaweeds and although this may seem to be of merely academic interest, many manufactured foods are thickened with a seaweed product, agar agar.

HOW TO INCREASE THE FIBRE IN YOUR DIET

There are a number of ways in which you can increase the fibre content of your diet:

Start using wholewheat bread instead of white bread – but make sure what you buy really is 100 per cent wholewheat and not just white bread coloured brown and 'enriched' with some of the goodness that should never have been taken away in the first place.

Use wholewheat flour for your baking. It really does make lovely pastry and can be used for cakes, biscuits, pancakes – I use it for all baking.

If you find wholewheat flour a bit strange to start with, mix it half and half with your normal flour, gradually increasing the amount as you get used to the texture and taste. Once you're accustomed to wholewheat flour, white flour seems so empty and tasteless – all I use it for is making modelling clay for my toddler!

Base your breakfast on a wholegrain cereal – or fruit – and if you think you're short of fibre add some bran as well. Turn to page 26 for more about breakfast.

Try to make sure that each meal includes at least one good source of fibre: potatoes in their skins, brown rice and other whole cereals, wholewheat bread and pastry, wholewheat pasta, plenty of vegetables and fruit.

As often as you can, try to base the main dish of your meal on a fibre food. This means using more vegetables, pulses and brown rice and there are plenty of delicious things you can do with them – see the recipe section of this book.

Serve fresh fruit for pudding, either just as it is or in something like a fool, compote or fruity muesli. This is another very

6

pleasant way to take fibre, along with vitamins, minerals and not too many calories. Again, more details in the recipe section.

Any of these suggestions will help you to increase the fibre in your diet. Use as many of them as possible, all of them if you can. But if for some reason you find it difficult, at least try to have wholewheat bread and to add a couple of tablespoonfuls of bran to your cereal each morning.

Normally it's a mistake, though, to think of fibre as something extra that you add to an otherwise normal diet. If you want to make your diet really healthy, the single most important thing to do is to start basing your meals on fibre foods. If the fibre content is right, the rest will follow: look after the fibre and the rest will take care of itself. Remember that research has shown that in the 'healthy' diets, the bulk of the day's calories comes from the fibre foods.

Talking of calories, you may well be wondering what all these fibre foods such as wholewheat bread and brown rice will do to your waistline. Actually these foods are not as high in calories as many people think. Look how they compare with other foods:

Food	Calories per 28 g (1 oz)
Wholewheat bread	63
Cooked rice	35
Breakfast oats	110
Baked beans	25
Cheddar cheese	120
Double cream	128
Sugar	110
Grilled bacon	120
Chocolate	150

In fact using fibre foods as the basis of your diet can help you both lose weight and stay slim, because they fill you up without supplying too many calories. If you have any further doubts, you only have to look at the slim figures of the people who base their diets on fibre – the rural Japanese or the natives in Africa, for instance. For more about slimming, see page 31.

Another thing which may concern you is whether eating a larger quantity of fibre will prevent you from getting enough protein and vitamins. This really isn't a problem, though. A varied diet based on fibre foods, as described in this book, will supply all the nutrients your body needs.

As far as protein is concerned, it now seems that many people, myself included, have in the past worried unnecessarily about this. The reason is that our daily protein requirements were previously thought to be far higher than they really are. Over the years the quantities recommended have decreased, so that the amount which the Food and Agriculture Organization of the United Nations (FAO) and the World Health Organization now give for an adult male – 36 grams of protein a day – is less than the 40 grams a day which, in 1948, a two year old was said to need!

An adult only needs to get 5 per cent of his day's calories from protein and wheat and cereals consist of 8–12 per cent protein; peas, and pulses after cooking, contain 6–7 per cent, and even potatoes contain about 2 per cent very good quality protein – so even if you based your diet entirely on these foods you would easily be able to meet your requirements. As it is, you would almost certainly be including other foods as well, some of which are more concentrated sources of protein.

So there is no difficulty as far as adults and older children are concerned. Where there could be a problem is in the case of very young children whose protein requirements are greater than their chewing ability. So they need some more concentrated protein foods such as cheese as well as the fibre foods. This is, however, much more likely to be a problem in the Third World than in the West, where most people, including children, eat far more protein than they need.

Finally, when people start eating more fibre foods they sometimes complain of feeling full and 'blown out'. This usually only lasts for a couple of weeks or so, maybe less, as their body adjusts. After that everything is usually fine and they begin to feel cleaner, lighter, better and generally healthier in a way that's difficult to describe.

Sugar – is it Really Bad?

The problem with sugar is really one of quantity. It's very easy to eat a large amount without realizing it.

When I say this to people they nearly always agree and add 'but I don't eat much sugar'. Yet sugar is put into so many foods that they're often surprised when they add up their daily total.

If you really want to know how much sugar you eat, you should keep a record for at least a week and then divide the total by the number of days to find your average daily intake. However even one day's total can give a rough idea. Try it now and see:

ADDED SUGAR (SUCROSE) IN COMMON FOODS

Food	Amount of Sugar (*Approx*)
2 sweet or chocolate biscuits	7 g ($\frac{1}{4}$ oz)
50 g (2 oz) chocolate bar	28 g (1 oz)
1 jam slice or doughnut	10 g ($\frac{1}{3}$ oz)
50 g (2 oz) slice of cake	20 g ($\frac{2}{3}$ oz)
35 g (1$\frac{1}{4}$ oz) frosted cereal	7 g ($\frac{1}{4}$ oz)
28 g (1 oz) cornflakes, plain	2·5 g ($\frac{1}{10}$ oz)
175 ml (6 oz) glass cola/soft drink	21 g ($\frac{3}{4}$ oz)
1 slice (100 g [3$\frac{1}{2}$ oz]) fruit pie	21 g ($\frac{3}{4}$ oz)
125 g (4 oz) tinned fruit	10 g ($\frac{1}{3}$ oz)
1 helping (60 g [2$\frac{1}{2}$ oz]) ice cream	15 g ($\frac{1}{2}$ oz)
28 g (1 oz) jam/marmalade	21 g ($\frac{3}{4}$ oz)
125 g (4 oz) jelly	21 g ($\frac{3}{4}$ oz)
125 g (4 oz) steamed pudding	38 g (1$\frac{1}{3}$ oz)
125 g (4 oz) instant whip dessert	20 g ($\frac{2}{3}$ oz)
150 g (5 oz) milk pudding, e.g. rice	15 g ($\frac{1}{2}$ oz)
1 rounded teaspoon sugar	7 g ($\frac{1}{4}$ oz)
150 g (5 oz) fruit-flavoured yoghurt	20 g ($\frac{2}{3}$ oz)

(Table adapted from *The Right Way to Eat* by Miriam Polunin, published by J. M. Dent & Sons Ltd.)

If you're eating less than about 28 g (1 oz) a day you've got nothing to worry about. Any higher than that – and 165 g (5½ oz) is the national average – and you could certainly improve your health by cutting down.

But surely you need some sugar for energy? That's what many people believe, but it's not so. There's nothing special about the 'energy' which sugar supplies. 'Energy' in this context is just another name for calories and, as all slimmers know, every food contains some of these.

Where sugar differs from other foods is that energy or calories is the only thing it does contain. With other foods, while you're taking in calories you're also getting valuable nutrients; with sugar, all you get is calories. This applies to brown sugar as well as white: although real brown sugar does contain some trace elements the quantity is so small as to be negligible.

You only need a certain number of calories a day and if you want to look and feel your best you should get these calories from foods which give you the maximum nourishment in return. The more calories you get from sugar the less room you've got for these other valuable foods.

Of course there's no need to be fanatical about this and a little sugar sometimes doesn't matter. But if you're eating anything near 165 g (5½ oz) a day it means you're using up about one-fifth of your daily calorie requirement and getting no nourishment in return.

If eating a lot of sugar is bad for adults, it's even worse for children – and it's not just their teeth which suffer. Young children need fewer calories so it's easier for sugar to occupy an even higher percentage of their day's total. This has been put as high as 25 per cent and even 50 per cent for some children, just at a time when they need all the nutrients they can get for building healthy bodies.

So what can you do about it? It's perfectly possible to cut down the amount of sugar you eat and finding ways to avoid it can become quite an exciting challenge.

The first thing to do is to look at what you eat during the day and see where the sugar is coming from. Is it sugar in tea and coffee? Soft drinks? Is your main sugar-intake at breakfast time, the sugar you have with your cereal and the marmalade you put on your toast? Or is it snacks and chocolates, puddings and cakes? Having found the main source or sources, the

10

next thing to do is to find ways of tackling the problem. Let's look at some of these.

WAYS OF REDUCING THE AMOUNT OF SUGAR YOU EAT

Sugar in tea and coffee: this can really add up alarmingly over the course of a day. You've only got to have four cups of tea or coffee each with a rounded teaspoon of sugar and that's 28 g (1 oz) of sugar straight away. More cups than this, or more spoonfuls of sugar in each, and you could easily be getting 2 or 3 ounces of sugar a day just from your drinks. Is it worth it?

Admittedly this is quite a difficult habit to break, but it can be done and there are three ways you might try it.

You can adopt the gentle approach: just reduce slightly the amount of sugar you put in. You probably won't notice much difference at first and if you persist you can gradually wean yourself off it.

That method works best for those who are methodical and persistent. If you like to see quick results, you'd probably find it easier to stop putting sugar into your drinks and give it up just like that. You will no doubt think it tastes awful at first and it will probably take you about a fortnight to get used to it. After that, if you get a sugared cup by mistake you will find it almost undrinkable. When that happens, you'll know you've won.

The third way of beating the habit is to use a substitute instead. Saccharine is the obvious one, though you may well prefer not to use it in view of some of the doubts concerning its safety. (In 1977 tests showed an increase in bladder cancer in rats who were fed with saccharine. The amounts given were far greater proportionally than we would ever eat and in any case we do not know that humans would respond in the same way as rats. However, in the USA the government took the report seriously and in Canada the government actually banned saccharine as a result of it.)

Honey is another possible substitute. Although it's really only sugar in another form, it's slightly lower in calories (80–90 calories in 28 g [1 oz] to sugar's 112) and its distinctive flavour means you can't put much into your drink without spoiling the flavour. But you should only really use honey as a temporary measure

11

to help you get used to a less-sweet taste – don't give up sugar only to get hooked on honey!

Sugar in soft drinks: this, like the sugar in tea and coffee, can really add up over the day because there's about 21 g ($\frac{3}{4}$ oz) of sugar in every glassful. Thirsty children who like their orange squash could quite easily be getting 100–125 g (3 or 4 oz) of sugar a day from this alone!

Yet orange squash is quite a modern invention. Before this came along, when children were thirsty they drank water. But if this idea doesn't appeal, soda water, Perrier and other mineral waters make a healthy alternative and so do real fruit juices (unsweetened), perhaps diluted half-and-half with water or soda water. They're lovely served very cold, with some lumps of ice.

Sugar on breakfast cereals: it's possible to use your whole day's 'allowance' of 28 g (1 oz) here, in one go, if you're not careful. Look for a cereal which doesn't have sugar amongst its ingredients and instead of eating it with sugar, add some chopped fresh fruit or a few raisins or dates. Again, it's largely a question of habit and if you persevere in a while you'll be surprised to find that you actually prefer your cereal without sugar. You may also find that you've lost quite a bit of weight without even really trying!

Jams, marmalade and other preserves: these contain a surprisingly high proportion of sugar – about 75 per cent. However, if you enjoy marmalade on your breakfast toast, and that's virtually all the sugar you have, I see no reason to deny yourself.

If, on the other hand, you're getting rather a lot of sugar from different sources and need to cut down where you can, there are various alternatives. You could try spreading your marmalade more thinly or use one of the excellent sugarless marmalades from health shops instead. You might also like to try one of the sugarless preserves I've given in the last recipe section of the book; you'll find recipes for a sugarless chutney and mincemeat there, too.

Puddings: when I started writing this book I thought that I would have difficulty finding enough recipes to make a section on sugarless puddings but I ended up with so many that the problem was deciding what to leave out. You really don't need to add quantities of sugar to your daily total in order to have a delicious pudding.

Cakes and biscuits: these can be a very big source of sugar and

I think you've got to make up your mind what place they've got in your diet. Of course again it's partly a question of quantity. There's a good deal of difference between someone who has the occasional cake or biscuit but otherwise eats little sugar, and the person who eats them frequently.

If you belong to the first group, I would say don't worry, although do remember the occasional cake when working out your average sugar intake.

On the other hand, if cakes and biscuits are an important part of your diet – and this may apply to children – then they are probably a major source of sugar and it would be worth finding something else to take their place. Exactly what depends on who is eating them, when and why. For instance if you find that you're regularly eating a sugary bun halfway through the morning because you have an 'energy gap', then either try and arrange things so that you get a better breakfast or be prepared with an apple or some nuts and raisins handy!

There are many 'convenience' snacks which aren't sugary: fresh fruit, nuts and raisins, peanuts, savoury biscuits, biscuits and cheese – and if you're at home, things like sticks of celery and scraped carrots (which I find often please children just as much as a biscuit).

If the problem is hungry children arriving home from school and wanting biscuits and cakes to fill them up, it's much better for them to have plenty of good wholewheat bread or scones or even fruit, nuts and raisins, yoghurt or perhaps a milk shake (see the drinks section) instead.

Can cakes and biscuits ever be considered healthy? Strictly speaking probably not, because even if they are made with the most wholesome ingredients, they still contain rather too much sugar and fat. However, to most of us, life would be dull indeed without the occasional cake or biscuit – and food must be joyful as well as healthy – so save them for weekends and special occasions. You might like to try some of the cakes and biscuits in the recipe section, made with wholewheat flour and just sweetened with dried fruit and small amounts of treacle and honey.

You will notice that I often suggest honey, fresh and dried fruit as sweet substitutes for sugar and you may wonder about the logic of this. These are, after all, sugar in another form and should be used with discretion. However treacle is a good source

13

of various nutrients, including iron, and though the nutrients in honey are probably too small to take into account, there's a naturalness about it that feels right to me. For this reason I see no harm in using small quantities for sweetening purposes. And it is also, as I've said before, slightly lower in calories than sugar.

When it comes to fresh and dried fruit, the reason why these are preferable to sugar is firstly, that they're nothing like as concentrated, and secondly that they offer other valuable nutrients in exchange for their calories.

You'd have to eat nearly 2 kilos ($3\frac{1}{2}$ pounds) of apples to get 165 g ($5\frac{1}{2}$ oz) of sugar and you'd also get a great deal else besides – fibre, vitamins, minerals and even protein.

Dried fruit varies in its calorie content according to the type but contains at most 75 calories to 28 g (1 oz) against sugar's 112. That's about one-third fewer calories and for this you get useful amounts of protein, iron, calcium (especially in figs), vitamin A in dried apricots and B vitamins in all the dried fruits.

The inclusion of vitamin B_1, thiamine, is particularly interesting because the body uses this when digesting sugar. Sugar, of course, doesn't contain thiamine, so in this case the body has to draw on the thiamine in other foods in order to digest the sugar. This is another good reason, in my opinion, for using dried fruit to sweeten food rather than sugar.

Fats and Cholesterol

Anyone interested in health knows that people who eat large quantities of animal fat are more likely to get heart attacks; that cholesterol is 'bad' and is found in egg yolk and that unsaturated fat is 'good' and is present in vegetable oils and some margarines.

But how do all these factors work together and what, if anything, should one do about them? Should you give up butter, cream and eggs? Is it worth using a polyunsaturated margarine? And what exactly is cholesterol, anyway?

Here are the facts as I understand them.

Let's start with cholesterol. Everyone has some cholesterol in their blood. It's a substance made by the body and is essential for certain functions.

Sometimes, though, the body starts to make too much and this is when it becomes a problem. As the blood circulates round the body some of the cholesterol in it forms a substance which coats the arteries. This can build up so much that it blocks the artery and causes clogging, or, in other words, arteriosclerosis. It can also crystallize in the gall bladder, forming gallstones.

The more cholesterol you've got in your blood, the more likely you are to have a heart attack, thrombosis or get gallstones.

So what is the danger level and how do you know if it applies to you?

Traditionally the level of cholesterol has been gauged by measuring the number of milligrams of cholesterol in one hundred millilitres of blood and is written as 'mg per cent'.

A reading of 120 mg per cent is low and safe while 275 mg per cent is considered to be the danger level with a high risk of heart attack. The average level for men in Britain and the USA is 230 mg per cent. This is an average, remember, so some will be higher and some lower. It is, however, rather too near the danger level for comfort – and one might say that it means most men are 'at risk'.

So what causes these high levels of cholesterol – and what can be done?

It used to be thought that the amount of cholesterol in our blood was increased by eating foods which contain it, like egg yolk. Now we know that eating such foods only accounts for a very tiny proportion of blood cholesterol. Most cholesterol is made by the body and seems to be related to the amount of fat we eat.

In Britain and America, where cholesterol levels are high, we get over 40 per cent of our daily calorie intake from the fat we eat. In southern Italy, where cholesterol levels are low, and where, until very recently, heart attacks were unknown, only 20 per cent of people's daily calorie intake came from fat. And in this country at the turn of the century, when heart attacks were also a rarity, it was nearer 10 per cent.

The Royal College of Physicians have recommended that we reduce our daily fat intake from 40 per cent to 35 per cent. In America the McGovern Committee has chosen 30 per cent as the goal. But if you're seriously interested in health, 15 or 20 per cent would be a better target for which to aim.

What does this mean in practice? It means you should try to limit your day's fat intake to not more than 56 g (2 oz). That sounds quite easy until you realize all the hidden sources of fat in a day's eating.

A glass of milk contains 11 grams of fat; 28 g (1 oz) of butter 23 grams; an egg 6·5 grams (10 grams if it's fried); 2 rashers of grilled bacon 12 grams and 56 g (2 oz) of sausage about 13 grams. That's already over 76 grams or nearly 3 ounces and all that could be eaten at breakfast!

The fat content of meat ranges from 2 grams per 28 g (1 oz) in chicken to 11 grams per 28 g (1 oz) for ham and pork, with lean beef and lamb at 5 and 6 grams respectively. Fried fish is around 3 grams and oily fish about 4 grams. Chips contain 2·5 grams of fat in every 28 g (1 oz); pastry, hard cheese, crisps, chocolate and ice cream all 10 grams and double cream 13·5 grams.

There is also a considerable amount of fat in cakes and biscuits: 56 g (2 oz) Dundee cake contains 9 grams of fat, chocolate sandwich cake 6 grams, a plain biscuit 1·5 grams, a chocolate digestive 3 grams and a shortbread finger 4·5 grams.

So as you can see it's not difficult to run up quite a high total and this will probably vary from day to day. The fluctuation doesn't matter. What is important is the overall average, and whether the fat is saturated or unsaturated.

Fats are classified according to their chemical structure and basically there are three types, saturated, monounsaturated and polyunsaturated. Animal fats, butter and cream, palm oil, coconut oil, some margarines and vegetable cooking fats are saturated. Olive oil is monounsaturated. Corn oil, sunflower seed oil and soya oil are unsaturated, as are some soft vegetable margarines (and these will say so if they are).

The strange thing is that while saturated fats appear to raise blood cholesterol, unsaturated fats seem to lower it. When this was first discovered some specialists recommended patients to eat large amounts of unsaturated fat. Now, however, the general opinion is that it's healthiest to replace saturated fats with unsaturated ones where possible but also to restrict fats generally.

Most of the fats mentioned in the foodstuffs which we looked at just now are saturated and if your daily intake is quite high you can immediately improve your diet by replacing them, where possible, with unsaturated fats, and reducing your total fats as much as possible. Here are some ways of achieving this; it is surprising how easy it is to put some of them into practice.

WAYS TO CUT DOWN ON SATURATED FATS

Try to concentrate on low-fat foods when planning your meals. Use the following, in which the fat content is so low as to be not worth counting:

Skimmed milk - you may be able to order this from your milkman or make it up from powder or granules;
Low-fat yoghurt;
Cottage cheese, fromage blanc and quark;
All fresh fruit except avocado pears which contain unsaturated fat (32 g in half a medium-sized one);
All fresh vegetables;
Dried lentils, peas and beans;
All cereals – rice, oats, barley, wheat, millet, rye – and products made from them without extra fat such as bread.

17

There are ideas for basing meals on these foods in the healthy eating through the day section and recipes for using them in the recipe chapters of this book.

Use skimmed milk instead of ordinary milk: if you find this difficult, try mixing skimmed milk half and half with normal milk; this way you can 'save' quite a worthwhile amount of fat over the week. I find it easiest to get liquid skimmed milk from my milkman and it's perfect for cooking as well as for using in tea and coffee etc. It's surprising how sickly and over-rich even silver top milk tastes once you're used to the clean, light taste of skimmed milk.

Use soft 'high in polyunsaturates' margarine instead of butter: again, you can mix it half and half with butter if you prefer. The flavours vary slightly, so try several and find the one you like best. My favourite is one called Vitaquell; you can get it at health shops. It's unsalted, and, I think, tastes rather like good unsalted butter.

Try to spread your bread thinly, whether you're using butter or margarine. Once again, we've found this is very much a question of habit and it's surprising how easily you can get used to a new one if you really want to.

Use a polyunsaturated oil for frying: this means corn oil, sunflower seed oil or soya oil. Try to fry food in the minimum of fat – and grill or bake foods instead where possible. Avoid fatty meats and base more meals on low-fat alternatives.

Make your own cakes and biscuits using polyunsaturated margarine: bought ones will almost certainly contain saturated fats.

Try making salad dressings with less oil or use some of the low-fat alternatives given in this book.

Stop buying cream, except perhaps for special occasions. There are some delicious, low-fat creamy toppings in the recipe section of this book.

Should you also limit the number of eggs you eat? Although egg yolk contains cholesterol, as I have already said, it now seems that the cholesterol we eat has very little effect on the cholesterol in our blood. In fact, as Colin Tudge points out in his book *Future Cook*, there are some people, the Spanish, for instance, who have always eaten quite a large number of eggs and yet until recently, when their diet changed in other ways, didn't get many heart attacks.

So it does not look as if eggs are harmful on their own. It is eggs-and-meat-and-butter-and-cream – and not many fibre foods – which would seem to cause problems. In other words, think of eggs as just another source of fat in the diet. In a diet already rich in fat they could be too much. But in a healthy, low-fat diet with plenty of vegetables and cereals, a few eggs are probably not harmful.

Should You Worry About Additives?

'Additives' are the substances which food manufacturers put into their products to make them taste and look as delicious as they can – and to ensure that they retain their attractiveness for as long as possible.

What additives manufacturers are allowed to use, and in some cases how much, are strictly controlled by government regulations, and any new substance has to undergo rigorous testing before it can be used.

Despite this, some people feel concerned about the situation as it is at the present time for a number of reasons.

Firstly, although any new additive has to satisfy certain very strict standards, there are still some rather dubious ones around.

This is because when the Food and Drugs Act, by which the use of additives is controlled, was introduced in 1955 it accepted many of the additives already in use. So these have not been subjected to the strict testing which additives have received since then.

Some of these original additives have now been withdrawn because tests have shown them to be potentially dangerous. But getting them tested and then banned if necessary is a lengthy process and in the meantime we, the consumer, are still buying and eating products which contain them.

A good example of this is Amaranth, a red food colouring which was one of the additives in use before the Act. In the late 1960s Russian additive testers published the results of research showing its link with birth deformities, still births and cancer in laboratory animals. In 1976 its use was banned in the USA after tests showed that it caused stunted growth and distorted the skeletons in chicken embryos. It is still widely used in the UK.

Secondly, additives can mount up. It is true that the quantity used in each foodstuff is often very small. However some additives are in such common use that it's quite possible to eat them many times a day in different foods.

Where additives are considered to be potentially harmful manufacturers are not permitted to exceed a certain specified amount. And these limits are said to allow a generous margin for safety.

However some of these restricted additives are amongst the most commonly used. Take sulphur dioxide, for instance. This is one of the most popular preservatives and is used in many foods ranging from dried fruit to tomato paste, wine and vinegar to jam.

You've only got to have sausages, instant mashed potato and a soft drink, for example, to have three lots of sulphur dioxide at one go. And if you follow that with bought apple pie or apple pie made with tinned pie filling, you've added some more.

Sulphur dioxide is known to destroy vitamin B_1 (thiamine), which is essential for the healthy functioning of the nervous system. So if you had many meals like the one above you could develop a deficiency of this vitamin, especially if you were also eating a good deal of sugar (see page 14).

This leads us to a third cause for concern: some additives interfere with the nutritional quality of food and with the body's ability to absorb certain vitamins and nutrients.

Other examples of this, besides sulphur dioxide, are glazing agents and calcium diosodium.

Glazing agents are oily substances which are used to make chocolates, sweets and dried fruits look shiny. They are known to prevent the body from absorbing fat-soluble vitamins.

Calcium diosodium is used during the canning process to prevent fruit and vegetables from darkening on contact with the air. It is thought to interfere with the body's ability to absorb some minerals.

Fourthly, in spite of tests and controls, there is still a great deal we do not know about what happens to additives after we have eaten them and what long-term effect they might have.

We do know that, in theory, some additives are changed into other substances in the stomach. We also know that the body does not always get rid of all the additives and that some of them can build up.

Sodium nitrate and sodium nitrite, which are found in many prepared meats and also in some cheeses, can be turned into nitrosamines. Under some conditions these are known to be cancer-inducing. So far this link between nitrates and nitrites and cancer is tentative and has not been proved, but it is something which needs watching.

Two other additives, butylated hydroxyanisole, known as BHA, and butylated hydroxytoluene, BHT, are known to accumulate in the body fat if eaten in substantial amounts.

These two substances are known as 'antioxidants' and used to prevent fats and oils from going rancid. They are put into some cooking fats and virtually all manufactured foods containing fats. In fact they're used so widely that it's easy to take in quite a large quantity from different foods during the course of a day.

Since BHA and BHT were introduced in the early 1950s there have been repeated fears concerning their safety. BHA has been found to stunt the growth of rats and to disturb the working of the muscles of the intestines in humans.

BHT has been widely tested in a number of different countries: results have indicated that it leads to liver and kidney damage; increase in blood fat and cholesterol; birth abnormalities, including major changes in the chemistry of the brain; also stunted growth and baldness. As a result, BHT has been banned in many countries.

In Britain, the UK Food Standards Committee has twice recommended (in 1958 and 1963) that BHA and BHT should no longer be used in food. Both are still extremely widely used, although not now in baby foods.

Lastly, no one knows how all the different additives eaten at one meal, or during the course of the day, will interact with each other, and what effect the whole mixture will have on the human body.

Having said all that, I do think it is important to keep a sense of proportion. We *are* talking about very small quantities, and although the use of additives is widespread – and increasing – there are nevertheless many foods which do not contain any additives at all. If these foods make up the main part of your diet you certainly minimize any risks and really needn't worry about the odd additive you might eat here and there.

FOODS WITHOUT ADDITIVES

The following foods are additive-free:

Fresh fruit and vegetables – but scrub fruit well to wash off any sprays and other preservative coatings

Dried peas, beans and lentils
Fresh meat and fish
Eggs
Cheshire and Cheddar cheese
Soft cheeses such as cottage cheese, curd cheese, 'fromage blanc' and quark, as long as they do not say 'with preservative' on the carton
Milk – ordinary, skimmed and UHT
Natural yoghurt and some fruit yoghurts – preservative, colouring and flavouring, if present, will be mentioned on the carton
Unsalted butter
Cold-pressed vegetable oils from health shops
Cereals – oats, wheat, rye, barley etc.
Wholewheat flour, also rye, barley, buckwheat and soya flour
Wholewheat bread if it's homemade or from a reliable health shop or small baker
Raw sugar, honey, treacle and molasses
Dates, figs and Sun Maid raisins; other dried fruits if bought from a health shop and sold as unsulphurated and untreated with mineral oil
Unsalted nuts, sunflower seeds, pumpkin seeds, sesame seeds, also unsweetened desiccated coconut
Fruit juice
Coffee and tea

As well as these there are quite a number of processed foods which are made with harmless additives, that is natural flavouring and colouring, and any of the following: agar agar, which is a seaweed product; lecithin, which occurs naturally in soya beans; edible gums, such as carob, acacia, ghatti, guar, tragacanth and karaya; and vitamin supplements.

Read the labels carefully and if necessary write to the manufacturers for more details. Heinz baked beans and tomato ketchup are two of my own storecupboard standbys which do not contain any harmful additives and there are many more.

All the recipes in this book are based on the foods in the additive-free list.

Is Salt Harmful?

One of the more bizarre discoveries of recent years has been that of the link between salt and high blood pressure. We all know that blood pressure rises as we get older, but should it – and need it? Research now suggests that it needn't, and it is salt which seems to be a key factor.

Experiments have shown that it is possible to raise the blood pressure of rats by giving them salt. The results were a little complicated because the effect of the salt took some time to show. They were also confusing because the actual quantity of salt given didn't seem to have any bearing on how quickly the blood pressure was affected or how high it rose.

As long as the rats were given a certain minimal dose their blood pressure would rise and after that more salt wouldn't make it go any higher. It was as if the salt acted as a kind of trigger mechanism and all that was needed was enough salt to set it off. And once the blood pressure had been raised, it wouldn't go down again, even if the salt was completely withdrawn from the rats' diet.

What did seem to affect the level of the rats' blood pressure was the age at which they started having the salt. The younger they were, the higher their blood pressure rose later.

Of course we cannot assume that salt will affect humans in the same way as it does rats, but the results of these experiments do compare interestingly with some studies undertaken by the late Professor Lot Page of Tufts University School of Medicine in Boston, USA.

Professor Page looked at the life style of a number of groups of people ranging from Australian to Chinese aborigines, from Congo pygmies to Greenland eskimos and others. These groups were linked by the fact that when the people studied were in their natural surroundings their blood pressure didn't rise with age. After a move to a city, however, their blood pressure did rise.

When he analysed the different life styles, Professor Page found that the one thing which they had in common was a diet which was very low in salt. Without exception, these people ate less than one gram of salt a day. This is very low indeed, considerably less than a patient in this country would have on a medically-prescribed low-salt diet where the allowance is usually 5 grams a day, about a level teaspoonful.

When you're used to the taste of salt it's not easy to cut down. But in view of the evidence it does seem worth making an effort to reduce your intake where you can. As with so many of these dietary questions, habit has a large part to play, and it is possible to get used to less highly-seasoned food.

While Professor Page was working on his research he did in fact try a low-salt diet and said that though it was difficult at first he got used to it fairly quickly. After he had been on this diet for about six weeks he found that salted food actually tasted unpleasant.

If you want to reduce your salt intake, I think it's best to do so gradually, just salting foods more lightly and not adding extra at the table. Although very many manufactured foods contain salt, some, such as the margarine mentioned above, do not and neither do the natural foods listed on pages 22–3. So if you make your meals mainly from these foods and watch the amount of salt you add, you can probably cut down quite a bit.

I certainly think it is important, in view of the findings above, to try and restrict the amount of salt which children eat. And if they get the taste for lightly-salted food when young perhaps it will be easier for them to keep to a low-salt diet later and remain healthy.

Healthy Eating Through the Day

So far we've considered individually various factors which can determine the healthiness of our diet. We have found that a healthy diet is:

high in fibre,
low in sugar and salt,
low in fat,
with as few processed foods as possible.

Now let's put all these principles together and see how they work in practice.

If it sounds complicated, don't worry, it's not as difficult as it appears. The reason is – and this is what is so satisfactory – all the factors work together. High-fibre foods are also unprocessed and if you're having plenty of them you don't need as much fat or sugar. Or, looked at from another way, if you cut down on fat and sugar and want to avoid processed foods, the natural ones to fill the gap are the high-fibre ones: fruits, vegetables, cereals.

So what kind of meals can you have? Let's look at a day of healthy eating.

BREAKFAST

In general it makes sense to keep breakfast as low in fat as possible to allow more scope for later in the day. If you like a cereal-based breakfast, you're halfway there. Just make sure you choose a cereal that's high in fibre and eat it with raisins, chopped fruit or grated nuts instead of lots of sugar.

If you like a cooked breakfast, you can still have one, but here you need to watch the fat. It's very easy to use up your whole day's 'ration' of fat at breakfast alone if you're not careful, and that's a bad start to anyone's day. Here are some ideas. I've given the calorie content so that you know where you are if you're watching your weight.

UNCOOKED BREAKFASTS

1. 175 g (5 oz) natural yoghurt (75 calories) with a chopped banana or 25 g (1 oz) raisins, sultanas or chopped dates (all about 75–80 calories), with, if liked, a tablespoonful of bran (15 calories) and/or a tablespoon of wheatgerm (25 calories), followed by a large piece of wholewheat toast with a scraping of margarine (100) and 2 teaspoons honey, marmalade (50 calories) or sugar-free marmalade (6 calories).
2. Continental breakfast: 2 pieces of toast as above or the equivalent in warm, crisp wholewheat rolls (200 calories), with honey, marmalade etc. as above.
3. A portion (25 g [1 oz]) of one of the wholewheat or bran cereals such as Weetabix, Grapenuts or Shredded Wheat (all around 100 calories) or All Bran (69 calories) with 25 g (1 oz) of raisins (75 calories) and 150 ml ($\frac{1}{4}$ pint) skimmed milk (50 calories), followed by toast as above if liked.
4. A portion of muesli mix (about 105 calories for 25 g [1 oz]) with skimmed milk (see above). Find a muesli mix which doesn't contain added sugar, or make your own from 450 g (1 lb) porridge oats (or a mixture of grains), 6 oz (175 g) each raisins and hazel nuts and 50 g (2 oz) wheatgerm. You can add a chopped apple or banana, too, if you like (50–80 calories) and follow with toast, as above.
5. Apple muesli: five ounces of natural yoghurt with a grated apple, half an ounce of porridge oats and half an ounce of raisins (200 calories), with toast to follow if liked.

COOKED BREAKFASTS

1. A poached egg on a large piece of wholewheat toast – unbuttered, or with just a scraping of margarine (180 calories).
2. Baked beans on toast: 225 g (8 oz) baked beans on a large piece of unbuttered wholewheat toast (300 calories).
3. An omelette: use 2 eggs to make the omelette and fry it in a teaspoonful of oil (200 calories).

4. Toasted cheese with tomatoes: a large piece of wholewheat toast with 50 g (2 oz) of grated Cheshire cheese, grilled and served with a large sliced tomato (310 calories).

5. Mushrooms on toast: 175 g (6 oz) button mushrooms fried in a teaspoonful of oil and served on wholewheat toast with just a scraping of margarine (150 calories).

6. Porridge made from 25 g (1 oz) oats and 150 ml ($\frac{1}{4}$ pint) water or skimmed milk and served with a teaspoonful of clear honey or maple syrup or a few raisins (about 200 calories with milk, 150 with water).

LUNCH

Lunch is only a problem really if you have to eat out because low-fat, high-fibre meals are not always easy to find. Salad is usually all right as long as it is not heavily dressed with mayonnaise or French dressing. Or a jacket potato, with grated cheese but without lots of butter. Baked beans on toast or an omelette are other possibilities.

It's much easier to get a healthy lunch, and to make sure that it fits in with the rest of your day's meals, if you make it yourself. Here are some ideas for packed lunches, quick lunches at home and 'sociable' lunches when you're joined by family or friends.

As with breakfast, except for special occasions, aim for plenty of fibre and not much fat.

PACKED LUNCHES

1. Wholewheat salad sandwiches: two large slices of wholewheat bread with just a scraping of margarine or butter (or try 'buttering' with cottage cheese or mustard) and filled with as much salad as you like and any of the following: 50 g (2 oz) cottage cheese, 25 g (1 oz) grated Cheshire cheese, a hardboiled egg mashed in a tablespoonful of natural yoghurt or cottage cheese or, if you eat meat, 50 g (2 oz) chicken (calorie counts vary but none are more than about 300 calories for a complete sandwich).

2. Celery sticks filled with 175 g (6 oz) cottage cheese, plus extra salad and an apple (230 calories).

3. A 125 g (4 oz) carton cottage cheese and lots of salad dressed

with lemon juice or low-calorie dressing if you like. Pack a fork to eat the cottage cheese with and finish with an apple, orange or pear (160 calories).
4. A carton of natural yoghurt, 25 g (1 oz) of hazel nuts, 15 g (½ oz) raisins and an apple (260 calories).
5. Easiest of all, just a handful of nuts and raisins and an apple (for 50 g [2 oz] of nuts and 25 g [1 oz] of raisins plus the apple, 322–480 calories, depending on type of nuts used – see calorie table).
6. A hardboiled egg, large piece of wholewheat bread scraped with butter and a piece of fruit (220 calories).
7. Ploughman's lunch: 125 g (4 oz) crusty wholewheat bread or roll filled with 25–50 g (1–2 oz) thinly sliced Cheshire cheese, sliced tomato, onion and gherkin (from 370–470 calories).

QUICK LUNCHES AT HOME

1. 175 g (6 oz) baked beans on a large piece of unbuttered wholewheat toast (250 calories).
2. A large bowl of home-made vegetable soup with a piece of unbuttered wholewheat bread (250 calories).
3. Piece of unbuttered wholewheat bread and 25–50 g (1–2 oz) Cheshire cheese (200–300 calories).
4. 175–225 g (6–8 oz) cottage cheese with sliced tomatoes or chopped cabbage mixed with low-fat salad dressing or lemon juice and 15 g (½ oz) raisins (215–275 calories).
5. An omelette made from 2 eggs cooked in a teaspoonful of oil (200 calories).
6. Any of the packed lunch ideas above.

SOCIABLE LUNCHES

These ideas are all based on dishes given in this book; refer to the recipe for calorie content.
1. Lentil soup, wholewheat rolls or bread, cheese board with several different cheeses, bowl of salad or a simple pudding such as ginger syllabub.
2. Quick bread pizza with lots of crisp green salad; orange and almond ice cream.

3. Creamy butter bean and avocado salad; pineapple and orange compote.
4. Macaroni and mushroom bake, tomato and watercress salad; fresh fruit.
5. Jacket potatoes, colourful mixed salad, grated cheese or cottage cheese; fresh fruit.

THE EVENING MEAL

Here are some ideas for healthy main meals based on recipes which you will find in this book.
1. Tasty brown lentil loaf with pineapple, baked potatoes, sprouts; apricot fool.
2. Green pepper and tomato bake, mashed potatoes, carrots with chopped parsley; baked apples with raisins and thick low-fat creamy topping.
3. Chinese vegetables with almonds, brown rice; apple snow.
4. Lentil dahl with brown rice and lots of extras to add: chopped banana, sliced tomato, mango chutney, roasted cashew nuts, desiccated coconut; green fruit salad.
5. Potato cakes, grilled tomatoes, mushrooms and perhaps a cooked green vegetable; honey muesli.
6. Mushroom flan, tossed green salad; fresh orange salad.
7. Pancakes stuffed with spinach and basil and baked in cheese sauce, carrots; coffee ice cream with maple syrup and walnuts.
8. Nutty brown rice with vegetables, watercress, lettuce and celery salad; fruit compote with ginger or tropical fruit salad.

Slimming

The health dangers of being overweight are often publicized – and no one wants to be carrying extra pounds around with them. Yet in spite of this, statistics show that half the population is above 'average', let alone ideal, weight.

The fact is it's not easy to slim and even harder to stay slim. But it can be done, and once you get to the right weight, an eating plan like the one described in this book will help you to stay there. If your diet is really healthy, you shouldn't put on weight – that's the theory, anyway.

In practice, life's not as simple as that. There are many pressures which can interfere with the best-planned diet.

Let's look at some of the difficulties and see if we can find any solutions.

First of all, whatever the problem, the most important thing is to have the right attitude of mind. You've really got to want to get slim. That's why it often helps to have an incentive, like a holiday, a new dress, the challenge of slimming with a friend, or just the constant thought in your mind of how lovely you will look and feel when you're beautifully slim and lithe.

Once you've got this motivation and determination, the next thing to do is to look at your present diet and life style to see why you are putting on or failing to lose weight.

If you've got the patience, it is a very good idea to write down everything you eat over a period of a week or so and add up the calories with the aid of the calorie counter at the back of this book.

Calorie requirements vary, but for most women 2150 calories a day are enough. A moderately active man needs 2750–2900 and both men and women need fewer calories as they get older and less active. A woman aged 55–74 needs only 1900 reducing to 1680 over the age of 75; a man aged 65–70 needs 2400 and only 2150 after the age of 75.

Some people can burn up calories very efficiently. Others do not have such a good metabolism and put on fat very easily. Once you become aware of the calorie content of what you eat you will soon find the number of calories which enables you to maintain an even weight.

Incidentally, don't be put off by the thought that you'll be constantly looking up the calorific values of foods. You won't. You will very quickly get to know the calorie-value of the foods you normally eat and then it will be just a question of looking up the odd item occasionally. Although there are many different diets, I am convinced that the most reliable method is counting calories.

Anyway, writing down what you eat – and drink – will enable you to see just where the calories are coming from. It may be that all you need to do is to adjust your diet slightly, first to lose the extra weight and then to reduce the calories in your normal diet so that you don't put it on again. On the other hand it could be that there are other pressures which are pushing you into fattening eating habits. So the next thing to do is to look at your life style and try and find out when and why you eat too much food, or the wrong foods.

Is it pressure of work which leads to lack of planning, so that you tend to grab a sugary snack because it's quick and easy? The answer here lies in better planning. With a little forethought you can have some delicious low-calorie snacks at the ready. Many of these are no more trouble than the more fattening ones, it's just that they do not always spring so quickly to mind.

Many of the quick lunches in the section on healthy eating through the day make excellent snacks. And you can't go far wrong with fruit, cheese, cottage cheese, hardboiled eggs, yoghurt, or wholewheat bread. If you can't buy them easily at work, try to take some with you so that you don't find yourself having to buy something calorific from the canteen.

Perhaps the problem isn't one of planning, but one of nibbling or eating compulsively through boredom or stress. A look at your life style will tell you when and why this usually happens.

Does your diet go to pieces because tension/tiredness make you need the comfort of food? If this is so, it is helpful to analyse the situations in your life which cause this to happen and think of ways of getting round them. Visualize yourself facing the problem and see yourself coping constructively without resorting to compulsive eating.

You can often beat this kind of 'tension eating' simply by relaxing. Even just consciously flopping your head down towards your chest and relaxing your neck muscles helps. It's difficult to eat compulsively when you're feeling relaxed.

And, as anyone who has beaten this compulsive eating problem will tell you, the urge passes quickly if you don't give in to it. Stave it off for five minutes while you relax or do something interesting, and you've won. Each time it gets easier as you break the habit.

It's tempting to eat for comfort when you're tired and maybe torn by all the conflicting needs of a demanding family. If this is your problem, try ten minutes in a hot bath, or alone, walking or relaxing flat on the floor. Stave it off for a few minutes and you've won. Another thing which helps is to clean your teeth. This is refreshing and also makes food taste unpleasant afterwards. Once you've made the initial effort, these are actually more reviving than eating a sugary snack – and none of them make you fat!

It may sound obvious, but if when you analyse things you find that you eat when you're bored, well, get yourself interested in something! Stock up with books from the library, take up sketching, carving, knitting, crochet – anything that you enjoy and for which you can feel some enthusiasm.

If social eating and drinking are the reason for your weight problem, you've either got to do what the Queen does and ration yourself to minimal portions, or arrange the rest of your eating so that you have enough calories in hand to allow for some treats, meals out and entertaining. But alcoholic drinks are high in calories and should be restricted to the occasional treat if you are really going to control the weight problem.

One of the nice things about slimming with the calorie method is that you can eat whatever you like, so you can 'budget' to some extent. On the other hand you could end up with a very unbalanced diet if you took this to excess. But you can take the occasional special meal in your stride by eating fewer calories on the preceding days. If you save 200 calories a day for 7 days you will have 1400 calories in hand. Of course this does mean scrimping a bit during the week – or accepting a higher daily total and slimming more slowly.

GETTING STARTED

The first thing to do is to put away your bathroom scales. You'll know if you're overweight and you'll soon feel the difference if you're losing weight.

To weigh oneself, even once a week, is in my opinion misleading. Weight tends to fluctuate from day to day and even hour to hour and it's very easy to get a false picture. So let your clothes be your guide and only get weighed after about four or six weeks – if you must.

Secondly, stop feeling deprived. Feel pleased and proud that you're actually doing something about the problem; and remember, after the first two or three days – certainly after the first week – it really does begin to get easier. Your stomach will shrink, you'll begin to feel slimmer and with each day that passes you'll be forming new, slim eating habits.

Enjoy the challenge of seeing how many ingenious ways you can find to cut down on calories. Forget about all the things you can't eat and concentrate on all the things you can eat. Congratulate yourself on your will-power and keep picturing yourself as slim and think how much better you will look and feel.

If you do find that your diet slips one day, don't give up. Look objectively at what it was that caused the breakdown and learn from it for the future. Think how you could have coped better and use this experience to help you to succeed another time.

PLANNING YOUR DIET

If you want to lose weight very quickly and are only a little overweight, you can aim for 800 calories a day at first to get you off to a good start, but don't keep this up for more than about a fortnight. 1000 calories is a better allowance; men will lose weight fairly rapidly on this, women a little more slowly – an average of two or three pounds a week.

Whatever your daily calorie allowance you can fill in the gaps with lots of vegetables which are so low in calories that you needn't bother to count them. This means all vegetables except dried pulses, peas, broad beans and sweetcorn, potatoes and sweet potatoes. Most fruits should be counted, but grapefruit can be eaten freely. Tea and coffee are also 'free', though don't forget to count the milk in your day's total.

It's often helpful, especially when you're starting to slim, to have plenty of things like celery sticks and scraped carrots ready so that

34

you can nibble away at these instead of being tempted by sweet things.

If you follow the ideas and recipes in this book, which are all calorie counted, you should not find it difficult to work out a scheme.

Most people find they eat roughly the same breakfast and it's quite easy to find several lunches which are within the calories allowed. Then you've only got to make sure that the evening meal is within the limit.

As I mentioned, you can often help yourself simply by getting organized beforehand. Plan your day's eating in advance as much as you can, so that you do not find yourself being pressurized by circumstances into having a more calorific meal than you'd really choose.

Some of the suggestions given in the healthy eating through the day section are low enough in calories for a slimming diet, but here are some more suggestions.

BREAKFAST

1. Two large pieces of wholewheat toast and just a scraping of butter or margarine (200 calories).
2. A carton of natural yoghurt (175 g [5 oz]) with 15 g ($\frac{1}{2}$ oz) raisins (112 calories).
3. One ounce of All Bran with 15 g ($\frac{1}{2}$ oz) raisins and 150 ml ($\frac{1}{4}$ pint) skimmed milk (156 calories) – or you could have Grapenuts, Shredded Wheat or Weetabix instead of the All Bran (190 calories with the raisins and milk).
4. Muesli: one ounce of rolled oats, a tablespoon each of bran and wheatgerm, 150 ml ($\frac{1}{4}$ pint) skimmed milk and half an ounce of raisins or a chopped apple (240 calories).
5. A large poached egg on unbuttered wholewheat toast or a boiled egg with a large piece of toast with a scraping of margarine (180 calories).

LUNCHES

1. A small carton (125 g [4 oz]) cottage cheese, lots of salad, an apple, orange or pear (160 calories).
2. Cheese sandwiches: two large slices of wholewheat bread

35

(unbuttered) with 75 g (3 oz) cottage cheese or 25 g (1 oz) Cheshire cheese (300 calories), or you can reduce the calories by having just 50 g (2 oz) bread with the cheese (220 calories).

3. An omelette, made from 2 eggs and cooked in 1 teaspoon oil (200 calories).

4. A medium-large jacket potato (175 g [6 oz]) with 15 g ($\frac{1}{2}$ oz) grated Cheshire cheese (200 calories).

5. Baked beans on toast: 175 g (6 oz) baked beans on a large piece of unbuttered wholewheat toast (250 calories).

6. An apple and a chunk (50 g [2 oz]) of Cheshire cheese (250 calories).

7. Raspberry milk shake, see drinks section, and an apple, orange or pear (170 calories).

8. Glass of fortified milk, again see drinks section (160 calories).

EVENING MEALS

You will find full details of all the dishes mentioned in the recipe section of this book.

1. Creamy tomatoes with horseradish; aubergine with mushroom and parsley stuffing, green beans, grilled tomatoes; fresh orange salad (270 calories).

2. Beetroot soup with creamy topping; stuffed jacket potatoes with a bowl of mixed salad; fresh fruit (350 calories).

3. Pink grapefruit with grapes; macaroni and mushroom bake with green salad or a lightly-cooked leafy green vegetable or courgettes; baked apples with raisins (340 calories).

4. Potato bake with crisp green salad or sprouts; apple, orange or pear (280 calories).

5. Creamy butterbean dip with crudités; stuffed aubergines in tomato and wine sauce, cauliflower and spinach; green fruit salad (370 calories).

6. Stuffed tomatoes; tasty lentil loaf with pineapple, spinach and grilled tomatoes; one piece of fresh fruit (350 calories).

7. Slice of mushroom flan with crisp salad; fresh fruit (280 calories).

8. Wedge of melon; green pepper and tomato bake with salad or cooked French beans; apple snow (310 calories).

9. Chinese vegetables with almonds; apple, orange or pear (350 calories).

Overcoming the Problems

In this section we're going to consider some of the questions which people often ask about the practicalities of eating for health. Does healthy food take longer to prepare, for instance, and are the ingredients more expensive to buy? Does it mean you must give up meat/wine/coffee/tea? And what about cooking for the family or dining with friends?

Let's look first at this question of time. People often say they'd like to make healthy meals but they can't because they're too busy: convenience foods are quick, cooking for health takes longer, they complain.

Yet many of the healthy foods really are just as quick to use as so-called convenience foods; think of eggs, cheese, fruit and wholewheat bread. Then there are the foods such as wholewheat pasta and brown rice which are no more trouble to prepare than the less healthy white versions, although you have to allow longer for the rice to cook.

There are many foods like these that are very quick, but the trouble is that when you're pressed for time you don't always think of them. I think it helps to make a list of quick, healthy meals and stick it inside one of the kitchen cupboards for inspiration.

Here's my own list of quick ideas for when I'm feeling tired/busy/lazy (the recipes and calorie counts are in the recipe section).

1. Jacket potatoes with grated cheese or cottage cheese and one of the easy-to-make salads such as tomato and watercress or cucumber, apple and raisin

2. A bean salad using tinned beans or ones I've managed to cook and put in the freezer, with warm rolls or fresh wholewheat bread and fresh fruit or a simple pudding like raspberry creams to follow.

3. Two or three nice cheeses with lots of good wholewheat bread or rolls, a pretty bowl of fruit, maybe some chilled wine and lots of good coffee.

4. Baked beans on wholewheat toast, tomato and onion salad; fresh fruit.

5. Quick bread pizza, cucumber and green pepper salad or celery and watercress salad; fresh fruit or one of the fruit salad mixtures.

6. Macaroni and mushroom bake with cooked green vegetable or frozen peas or crisp green salad; fruit.

7. Risotto with green salad; fresh fruit or fresh orange salad.

8. Lentil soup, good wholewheat bread, cheese, plenty of fruit and some nuts, dates and raisins.

9. Vegetable casserole, with a side salad or an extra cooked vegetable if you've got time; fresh fruit or yoghurt to follow.

10. Wholewheat spaghetti tossed in olive oil, seasoned with plenty of freshly-ground black pepper and served with some dry grated Parmesan cheese and a tomato or green salad; fresh fruit.

11. Spicy lentil dahl with sambals; fruit.

12. Potato bake – this is quick to prepare but takes 1½ hours to cook – with spinach and grilled tomatoes.

13. Cheating gnocchi, green salad or quickly-cooked green vegetables; pineapple and orange compote.

14. Aubergine casserole with jacket potatoes, brown rice or spaghetti and a little grated cheese or roasted nuts; baked apples with raisins.

15. Green pepper and tomato bake, Bircher potatoes, cauliflower and/or sprouts or green beans; fresh pears.

16. Chinese vegetables with almonds; fresh fruit.

17. Butter beans and mushrooms in creamy sauce, watercress, lettuce and celery salad; apples.

18. Spiced lentils with rice, cabbage and pineapple salad; yoghurt, ginger syllabub or fresh fruit.

19. Wholewheat spaghetti with lentils and red pepper, fennel or celery and cucumber salad; oranges.

20. I don't do many omelettes or eggy dishes because they're not very popular with my family, but eggs are a real convenience food and if you like them you could add omelettes and other egg dishes to this list.

Those are the recipes which I consider to be particularly quick to make, but I have not included any recipes in this book which are complicated or too time-consuming.

Although I use mostly fresh vegetables, I do use frozen vegetables sometimes and also the occasional can, particularly canned tomatoes, pineapple canned in its own juice and, from time to time, canned red kidney beans, chick peas or butter beans. But with the beans I usually cook 500 g (1·1 lb) at a time, divide them into five portions and freeze them. To save time I also often make double or triple batches of our favourite dishes and freeze them: I have given freezing notes with the recipes.

I know that if you're very health-conscious you may not approve either of the occasional tin or of the deep freeze and I have given alternatives in the recipes. But these are short-cuts which I do not think detract from the overall healthiness of the food and which, as far as I am concerned, make it practical in a busy life.

Some of the healthy foods such as wholewheat bread and brown rice cost more than their refined counterparts and because of this people often ask whether this style of eating is more expensive. But though you spend extra on these whole foods and on fruit and vegetables you can offset this with the saving made by eating more potatoes, bread, rice and pulses instead of meat and fish.

So although at first glance a healthy diet may seem more expensive, in practice I don't think it is. And if you really have to economise, you can do so very healthily by basing more of your meals on potatoes, brown rice and wholewheat bread and serving less of the concentrated protein foods such as meat, cheese and eggs. (If you think this sounds fattening see page 7!)

What about drinks? Can you still have tea, coffee and wine? I think the word here is moderation. Although both tea and coffee contain caffeine, which stimulates the heart and increases mental alertness, there is no evidence to suggest that they're harmful in reasonable quantities.

Both tea and coffee can occasionally provoke allergies, as indeed can many other foods, ranging from milk, eggs and cheese to wheat, tomatoes, oranges and yeast. (For more information about this see *Eating and Allergy* by Robert Eagle [Futura].) If you are allergic to tea and coffee obviously you will want to replace them either with decaffeinated coffee and low caffeine tea or with one of the cereal coffee substitutes and herb teas (all from health shops). But for most people tea and coffee are fine as long as they're not taken to excess.

The same goes for wine and beer although, as with so many foods, these tend to contain more additives than they did. So go for real ale and traditionally-produced (or home-made) wines. Alcoholic drinks are quite high in calories, so you can't drink much if you want to get or keep slim and healthy. But I don't think the occasional glass does any harm.

If you like eating out, or often eat with friends, you may wonder how things work out when you're trying to adopt a healthy way of eating.

When I eat out I just try to pick the healthiest meal available. Not because I feel I must, more because when you're used to whole, healthy foods, anything less tastes empty. Wholefood and vegetarian restaurants are a good bet; in ordinary restaurants look for the least processed and least fatty dishes.

What you do about eating with friends depends on your personality and attitude – and the friends. Speaking for myself, the one thing I dislike about being a vegetarian is the fact that it can be a bit of a nuisance for other people. So in the case of the odd meal with friends I would never make a fuss about wholewheat flour, etc. as well! Actually I think that having the occasional meal that's perhaps less than healthy can sometimes be a good thing, preventing, let's hope, any fanaticism creeping in.

Another question which people often ask is how they can get the family to eat healthy foods. But why do people always assume that the children and 'the family' won't like the healthy foods? Why shouldn't they like them? They're far more tasty than the white alternatives.

I know that food is a question of habit – but if you're using this argument against whole foods, you can also use it in their favour, for you can surely acquire the habit for whole foods in the same way as you've acquired the habit for processed foods.

Having said that, I do realize that some families can be rather difficult about trying anything new, and the only way here is to introduce the healthy foods gently, mixing white flour with wholewheat flour, butter with polyunsaturated margarine, ordinary milk with skimmed milk and introducing as many healthy dishes as possible alongside old favourites. You can also make dishes healthier in ways which make little difference to their taste or appearance: using less fat in soups, salad dressings and sauces, for instance, and making pastry, cakes and biscuits with polyunsaturated margarine.

How much you want to or are prepared to change your cooking and eating habits, and those of your family, is of course a personal matter. But everyone wants to look and feel their best – bright-eyed and full of energy and able to do the things they want to do, to live life to the full. If, by making one or two changes in your cooking and eating habits while still enjoying good food, you can make this more likely to happen, isn't it worth a try?

The Recipes

Soups

A bowl of soup is comforting and warming and can fill you up for surprisingly few calories.

The main difference between an ordinary soup and a healthy one lies in the amount of fat used in the preparation.

If you were being very health-conscious, you probably wouldn't use any at all, but I think that frying the vegetables first in a little oil really does make a difference to the result, without adding too much to the calories. You could leave out this process though, if you prefer, and just put the vegetables straight into the saucepan with the stock or water.

To garnish the soup, instead of using cream, try thinning a little fromage blanc with milk and swirling this over the top (see beetroot soup) – the effect is stunning and when I have done it no one has yet realized it's not real cream. Chopped fresh green herbs, when they're available, are fresh-tasting and pretty snipped over a bowlful of pale-coloured soup, and for something crunchy cut crisp toast into dice and sprinkle these over the soup at the last moment.

All these soups are quick and easy to make and some of them are substantial enough to make a simple meal with just some warm, crusty wholewheat bread or rolls, fruit and perhaps a little cheese.

BEETROOT SOUP

This is a beautiful ruby red soup that looks mouthwatering with its swirl of creamy white topping. In hot weather this soup is also very good served chilled

Serves 4
Calories: 144 in each serving, including topping

1 onion
1 large potato – about 225 g
  (8 oz)
1 tablespoon vegetable oil
450 g (1 lb) cooked beetroot –
  get the kind that is still in
  its skin, not beetroot which
has been peeled and
  preserved in vinegar
1·2 litres (2 pints) water
Sea salt and freshly ground
  black pepper
1 tablespoon lemon juice

For the topping:
1 tablespoon fromage blanc

2 tablespoons liquid skimmed
  milk

Peel and chop the onion; peel and dice the potatoes. Heat the oil in a fairly large saucepan and fry the onion, without browning, for about five minutes, then add the potatoes, turn them in the oil and cook gently for about 5 minutes more. Meanwhile slip the skin off the beetroot and dice the flesh. Add the beetroot to the saucepan and stir in the water or stock. Bring up to the boil then leave the soup to simmer, with a lid on the saucepan, for about 20 minutes until the potatoes are soft. Liquidize the soup, then return it to the saucepan and flavour with salt, pepper and the lemon juice. Reheat gently. Make the topping by blending the fromage blanc with the milk until it is the consistency of thick pouring cream. Swirl a little of this over the top of each bowlful of soup just before serving.

TO FREEZE: cool and pour into a rigid container, allowing a little room for expansion. To use, thaw overnight, reheat gently.

LEEK SOUP

You can liquidize this soup, leave it as it is, or liquidize half or two-thirds and leave the rest to give some texture. The soup has a delicious, delicate flavour just as it is, but if you want to make it taste more creamy, stir two tablespoons of fromage blanc into it just before serving, as described for potato soup.

Serves 4
Calories: 155 in each serving; or 160 if adding the fromage blanc

450 g (1 lb) potatoes	Sea salt and freshly ground
2 medium-sized leeks	black pepper
1 tablespoon oil	1 tablespoon chopped parsley
850 ml (1½ pints) water or	
light stock	

Peel and dice the potatoes; trim, thoroughly wash and slice the leeks. Heat the oil in a fairly large saucepan and add the potatoes and leeks. Turn them in the oil for a couple of minutes, being careful not to let them get brown. Stir in the water or stock. Bring up to the boil then leave the soup to simmer, with a lid on the saucepan, for about 20 minutes, until the vegetables are cooked. Liquidize some or all of the soup as desired, then season and reheat. Sprinkle the parsley over the top of each portion just before serving.

TO FREEZE: cool, pack in a rigid container leaving space for the soup to expand as it freezes. To use, thaw out completely then reheat gently, stirring often.

LENTIL SOUP

I think this smooth, golden soup is the most comforting of all. It is also extremely easy to make, nourishing and high in fibre. It was the first solid food I gave my toddler when she was six months old and she still adores it – in fact it's a great favourite with everyone. The soup takes about 15 minutes to make from start to finish with a pressure-cooker, about 30 minutes without, and, with wholewheat bread or rolls, makes a filling meal.

Serves 4
Calories: 205 in each serving

1 large onion, peeled and chopped	1 litre (1¾ pints) stock or water
1 tablespoon oil	Sea salt and freshly ground black pepper
225 g (8 oz) split red lentils	

Heat the oil in a fairly large saucepan and fry the onion for about 5 minutes, until it's lightly browned. Add the lentils and water and bring up to the boil, then leave the soup to simmer gently for about 20 minutes, or pressure-cook for 5 minutes, until the lentils are soft and beige-gold. Liquidize the soup, season well with salt and plenty of black pepper and reheat before serving. You can sharpen the flavour with a little lemon juice and vary the flavour by adding some crushed garlic and/or chopped green herbs just before serving. Another pleasant variation is to flavour with a spoonful of curry powder and serve with a circle of lemon floating in each bowl.

TO FREEZE: cool soup and pour into a rigid container. To use the soup, thaw overnight, reheat gently.

GOLDEN ONION SOUP WITH CHEESE

I don't quite know why, but this soup always makes me feel festive; maybe it's because I associate it with happy times in France or perhaps it's something to do with the sherry. Anyway, it makes a lovely winter lunch or late-night supper and although it's filling, it's not too high in calories.

Serves 4
Calories: 250 in each serving

450 g (1 lb) onions	1 large clove garlic, peeled and crushed
1 tablespoon oil	
1 tablespoon flour	4 teaspoons Dijon mustard
850 ml (1½ pints) water	Sea salt and freshly ground black pepper
1 vegetable stock cube	
3 tablespoons cheap sherry	

To serve:
4 slices wholewheat bread
100 g (3–4 oz) cheese, grated

Peel the onions and slice them into fairly thin rings. Heat the oil in a large saucepan and fry the onions slowly for 15–20 minutes, until they're golden, stirring them from time to time. Add the flour and cook for a few seconds before putting in the water, stock cube, sherry, garlic, mustard and a seasoning of salt and pepper. Bring mixture up to the boil, then let it simmer gently for 30 minutes. Just before the soup is ready, warm four heatproof soup bowls and lightly toast a slice of bread for each; put the toast, roughly broken up, into the bowls. Prepare a moderately hot grill. When the soup is ready, check the seasoning, then ladle it into the bowls, scatter the grated cheese on top and place the bowls under the grill to melt the cheese; serve immediately.

TO FREEZE: unsuitable.

POTATO SOUP WITH FRESH HERBS

Although this is a simple soup, it always tastes good, with its smooth creamy texture and topping of fresh green herbs. You can make the soup even creamier by adding the fromage blanc, rather as you would add cream, and you can also swirl some over the top of the soup, as in the beetroot soup recipe, for an attractive garnish.

Serves 4
Calories: 150 in each serving with fromage blanc, 135 without

1 tablespoon vegetable oil
1 onion, peeled and chopped
450 g (1 lb) potatoes, peeled and diced
900 ml (1½ pints) water
Sea salt and freshly ground black pepper
2 tablespoons fromage blanc – optional

2 tablespoons chopped fresh herbs – whatever you can get – tarragon, chervil or lovage are particularly good, or parsley and/or chives

Heat the oil in a fairly large saucepan and fry the onion for 3–4 minutes, stirring often – don't let it get brown. Then add the potato and stir over the heat for a further 2–3 minutes. Pour in the water, bring up to the boil and leave to simmer for about 15 minutes, until the potatoes are tender. Liquidize or sieve, then season with salt and pepper. Reheat, stir in the fromage blanc if you're using it and serve sprinkled with the herbs.

TO FREEZE: cool, pour into a rigid container allowing space for expansion and freeze. To use, allow to thaw thoroughly then reheat gently.

EASY TOMATO SOUP

If, like me, you include canned tomatoes amongst your permitted convenience foods, they can be made into a very quick soup. Actually this soup can also be made from fresh tomatoes; just wash them and put them in, skins and all, but sieve the soup after liquidizing.

Serves 4
Calories: 130 in each serving

1 onion, peeled and chopped	1·2 litres (2 pints) water
350 g (12 oz) potatoes, peeled and cut into dice	Sea salt and freshly ground pepper
1 tablespoon oil	A dash of honey
425 g (15 oz) can tomatoes or 450 g (1 lb) fresh	Chopped parsley or chives

Fry the onion and potato in the oil in a fairly large saucepan for about 5 minutes, stirring often, but don't let them brown. Add the tomatoes and water, bring to the boil, then leave to simmer for 15–20 minutes, until the potato is cooked. Liquidize the soup and return it to the rinsed-out saucepan.

Season with salt, pepper and just a little honey if you think it needs it. Serve with a little fresh parsley snipped over the top.

TO FREEZE: cool and pour into a rigid container. Allow several hours for thawing; reheat gently.

WATERCRESS SOUP

This is an easy soup to make and is fresh-tasting and delicious. It is very good with the creamy topping given in the recipe for beetroot soup.

Serves 4
Calories: 140 in each serving

1 bunch watercress
1 onion, peeled and chopped
450 g (1 lb) potatoes, peeled and diced

1 tablespoon oil
850 ml (1½ pints) water
Sea salt and freshly ground black pepper

Wash the watercress carefully, separating the stalks from the leaves; chop the stalks roughly. Heat the oil in a large saucepan and add the onion; cook gently for 5 minutes but don't let it get brown, then put in the potato and watercress stalks (keep the leaves on one side for later). Stir the vegetables over a gentle heat for a minute or two so that they all get coated with the fat, then pour in the water, bring the mixture up to the boil and let it simmer gently for about 15 minutes or until the potato is soft. Put the soup into the liquidizer goblet together with the watercress leaves and a little salt and pepper and blend until smooth. Check seasoning; reheat gently.

TO FREEZE: unsuitable.

WINTER VEGETABLE SOUP

This is a lovely winter soup, filling and nourishing yet light in texture and delicate in flavour. If you serve big bowls of it with home-made bread, cheese and fruit, it makes a complete meal, but it's also good as a first course on a cold day.

Serves 4
Calories: 156 in each serving

1·2 litres (2 pints) water
2 fairly large carrots
2 onions
2 medium-sized potatoes
1 swede – about 225 g (8 oz)
1 turnip – about 225 g (8 oz)

4 sticks celery
15 g ($\frac{1}{2}$ oz) polyunsaturated
   vegetable margarine
Sea salt and freshly ground
   black pepper

Put the water into a large saucepan and bring to the boil while you prepare the vegetables, cutting them into fairly small chunks; add them to the water, together with some salt, and simmer gently, with a lid on the saucepan, until they're all tender – about 30 minutes.

Scoop out two big ladlefuls of the soup and liquidize or mouli it with the margarine, then pour it back into the saucepan and stir it into the rest of the soup. This thickens the soup while the pieces of whole vegetable give it body and interest. Check the seasoning, adding a little more salt if necessary and grinding in some black pepper, then reheat the soup before serving.

TO FREEZE: cool and store in a rigid container. To use, allow to thaw overnight; reheat gently.

CHILLED CUCUMBER SOUP

This refreshing chilled soup makes a beautiful light, low-fat starter.

Serves 4
Calories: 66 in each serving

1 cucumber
425 g (15 fl oz) natural
  yoghurt
8 sprigs mint

4 sprigs parsley
1 teaspoon sea salt
4 sprigs mint to garnish

Peel the cucumber, then cut it into rough chunks. Put the chunks into the liquidizer goblet with the yoghurt. Wash the mint and parsley and remove the stalks; add the leaves to the cucumber and yoghurt together with the salt. Blend at medium speed until you've got a smooth purée. Transfer the purée to a bowl and place it in the fridge until it's really cold. Check the seasoning and add more salt if necessary – chilling tends to dull the flavour – then serve the soup in individual bowls with a sprig of mint floating on top of each.

TO FREEZE: unsuitable for freezing.

CHILLED YOGHURT AND SPRING ONION SOUP

Cool, creamy-tasting natural yoghurt and spring onions make a beautiful chilled soup that's not nearly as strange as it sounds and couldn't be easier to make.

Serves 4
Calories: 90 in each serving

425 g (15 fl oz) natural yoghurt
300 ml ($\frac{1}{2}$ pint) skimmed milk
9–12 spring onions, washed, trimmed and chopped
Sea salt and freshly ground black pepper

Put the yoghurt into a large bowl and stir in the milk. Add the spring onions and season to taste. Chill until ready to serve. If you keep the yoghurt and milk in the fridge they will of course be already chilled when you mix them and the soup can be served straight away – an almost instant soup.

TO FREEZE: unsuitable.

HEALTHY VICHYSSOISE

I love vichyssoise and so I wanted to make a healthy version without the cream. Instead, I used that lovely white cheese, fromage blanc, which has a smooth texture and tastes creamy yet

53

is low in fat and only contains the same number of calories as cottage cheese. Whilst I don't think this soup is quite as luxurious-tasting as a real vichyssoise, it is very pleasant and creamy and people seem to enjoy eating it.

Serves 4
Calories: 195 in each serving

450 g (1 lb) potatoes
2 medium-sized leeks
1 tablespoon sunflower or
   corn oil
850 ml (1½ pints) water or
   light stock

125 g (4 oz) fromage blanc
Sea salt and freshly-ground
   black pepper

To finish:
1 tablespoon fromage blanc
2 tablespoons liquid skimmed
   milk

1 tablespoon chopped chives

Make the soup exactly as described for leek soup on page 46, but liquidize all the soup, together with the fromage blanc. Season well with salt and freshly-ground black pepper. Chill. If the soup seems rather on the thick side after chilling, thin it with a little icy cold water and check seasoning. To make the topping, mix the tablespoonful of fromage blanc with the milk until smooth. Spoon the soup into individual bowls, swirl the creamy fromage blanc mixture over the top of each and sprinkle with chopped chives. Serve with warm wholewheat rolls or bread.

TO FREEZE: make the leek soup but don't add any fromage blanc. Freeze the soup in a rigid container. To use, let the soup thaw out overnight then put it into the liquidizer with the 125 g (4 oz) fromage blanc and blend until smooth and creamy. Check seasoning and chill before serving as described above.

First Courses

A first course doesn't need to contain lashings of oil, butter and cream to be good. All the ones in this section are fairly low in calories yet are refreshing and always seem popular. They are based on fresh fruits, vegetables and pulses, with low-fat creamy cheese or yoghurt and small quantities of olive oil to give richness and flavour.

With the exception of hummus and the creamy butter bean dip, these dishes don't freeze well; however, they are all quick and easy to make.

AVOCADO DIP

I don't know whether it has something to do with the fact that everyone is eating with their fingers, but I find a meal always seems to get off to a particularly friendly, lively start when I serve a dip, and this is a specially good one. Incidentally, although no one could call avocados low in fat, the oil which they contain is polyunsaturated. And as they are so very delicious, and rich in vitamins, I see no harm in using them, balancing their fattiness by serving them with other dishes which are low in fat.

Serves 6
Calories: 255 in each serving

250 g (8 oz) fromage blanc
1 clove garlic, crushed
Sea salt, pepper and tabasco

2 large, ripe avocados
1 tablespoon lemon juice
A little wine vinegar

To serve:
Crisp wholewheat toast, or crudités as in the cream cheese dip recipe

55

Mix together the fromage blanc, garlic and some salt, pepper and tabasco. Just before serving, peel and mash the avocados with the lemon juice; add to the creamy cheese, mixing well. Check seasoning, adding a dash of wine vinegar.

TO FREEZE: unsuitable.

AVOCADO AND MUSHROOM SALAD WITH BROWN BREAD AND BUTTER

This is a pleasant mixture of flavours, textures and colours.

Serves 4
Calories: 205 a serving, without the bread and butter – allow 80 calories for a thin piece of very lightly-buttered bread

1 large ripe avocado pear	1 tablespoon wine vinegar
2 tablespoons lemon juice	Salt and pepper
450 g (1 lb) very fresh white button mushrooms	A few chopped chives
1 tablespoon best quality olive oil	

To serve:
Lightly buttered brown bread

Cut the avocado in half and remove the stone and peel. Slice the flesh and sprinkle with the lemon juice. Wash and thinly slice the mushrooms. Put the mushrooms into a bowl with the avocado and add the oil, vinegar and some salt and pepper. Mix everything together lightly. Serve on individual dishes with some chives snipped over the top.

TO FREEZE: unsuitable.

CREAMY BUTTER BEAN DIP

If you use tinned butter beans, or ones that you have previously cooked and frozen, this can be made in no time and is smooth and delicious. I love the flavour of butter beans and olive oil together.

Serves 4
Calories: 100 in each serving, without olives and toast

100 g (3–4 oz) butter beans, soaked and cooked, or a 425 g (15 oz) can
1 tablespoon olive oil
1 teaspoon wine vinegar

1 garlic clove, peeled and crushed
Sea salt and freshly ground black pepper

To serve:
A few black olives, crisp wholewheat toast

Drain the butter beans, keeping the liquid. Put all the ingredients into the liquidizer goblet with 2 tablespoons of the liquid. Blend to a smooth purée, adding a little more liquid if necessary to make a thick but creamy consistency. Spoon into a pâté dish, fork the top and decorate with a few black olives. Chill before serving.

TO FREEZE: this freezes well in a small container. To use, thaw completely, then beat until creamy.

CREAM CHEESE AND HERB DIP
WITH CRUDITÉS

For the crudités I think it's nice to serve a selection of two or three fresh vegetables: cauliflower sprigs, small strips of red or green pepper, fingers of scraped carrot, spring onions or radishes, just washed and trimmed with the green part left on if it's presentable, sticks of crisp celery or chicory.

Serves 6
Calories: 60 in each serving

250 g (8 oz) fromage blanc
150 g (5 fl oz) natural yoghurt
1 garlic clove, peeled and
   crushed
2 tablespoons finely chopped

green herbs – chives,
parsley or whatever is
available
Sea salt and freshly ground
black pepper

To serve:
A selection of vegetables as
   above

Put the fromage blanc into a bowl and stir in the yoghurt, garlic and herbs and mix to a smooth consistency. Season with salt and pepper. Spoon the dip into a serving dish and chill until required. Arrange the crudités around the dip or put them into bowls and serve with the dip.

TO FREEZE: unsuitable.

CREAMY CARROT SALAD WITH WHOLEWHEAT ROLLS

To make the roasted hazel nuts for this recipe, spread out some hazel nuts on a dry baking sheet and bake them in a moderate oven until the skins will rub off and the nuts underneath are golden. This takes about 20 minutes and makes such a difference to the flavour of the nuts. You can either leave the brown outer skins on or rub them off and if you like hazel nuts it's worth doing 225 g (8 oz) or even 450 g (1 lb) at a time. The hazel nuts give a crunchy texture to this creamy golden salad; it's delicious eaten with warm wholewheat rolls.

Serves 4
Calories: 135 in each serving without rolls

350 g (12 oz) finely grated
    carrot
2 tablespoons natural yoghurt
125 g (4 oz) curd cheese
2 teaspoons olive oil

½ teaspoon wine vinegar
25 g (1 oz) raisins
25 g (1 oz) roasted hazel nuts
Sea salt and pepper

To serve:
Warm wholewheat rolls

Put the grated carrot into a bowl and mix in all the other
ingredients. Serve piled up in a pottery dish and let everyone help
themselves, eating the salad with the rolls.

TO FREEZE: unsuitable.

PINK GRAPEFRUIT WITH GRAPES

Grapefruit seems such an easy, unimaginative starter that for
years I hardly ever served it. Yet it's excellent from the health point
of view, being very low in calories and it's refreshing and popular
with most people. And the red grapefruits with their juicy pink
flesh are much sweeter than the others and look delightful. So here
is a way of serving them in which the pink of the grapefruit is
enhanced by the deeper colour of the grapes – the effect is very
pretty.

Serves 4
Calories: 45 in each serving

2 pink grapefruits
175 g (6 oz) black or red
    grapes, halved and stoned

Cut the grapefruits in half as usual, then scoop out all the flesh
and remove pieces of skin and any pips. Add the grapes to the
grapefruit flesh and mix together. Pile grapefruit and grape
mixture back into the grapefruit skins and place in individual
bowls.

TO FREEZE: unsuitable.

HUMMUS

Chick peas have such a beautiful flavour that I think it's a pity to overpower it by adding a great deal of tahini: I like it best when you can taste both flavours distinctly. You can always increase the quantity of tahini if you like, but don't forget to allow for the extra calories if you're slimming: it's 90 calories for a teaspoonful. If you use canned chick peas for this dip – or ones you've previously cooked and frozen – it can be made very quickly.

Serves 4
Calories: 155 for each serving

100 g (3–4 oz) chick peas, soaked and cooked – or use a 425 g (15 oz) can
1 garlic clove, peeled and crushed
1 tablespoon lemon juice
1 teaspoon tahini (sesame cream – from health shops)
2 tablespoons olive oil
Sea salt
Paprika pepper

Drain the chick peas, keeping the liquid. Put the chick peas into the liquidizer goblet with 5 tablespoons of the reserved liquid, the crushed garlic, lemon juice, sesame cream and half the olive oil and blend to a smooth purée. An alternative way to make this is to sieve the chick peas and then mix them with the remaining ingredients, as above, and beat until smooth. Season mixture then spoon it into a small bowl or divide between individual plates and smooth into a flat shape. Fork over the surface and sprinkle with the remaining olive oil and some paprika.

TO FREEZE: hummus freezes very well and is handy to have ready. Freeze in a small container; to use, thaw completely then beat until smooth.

MARINATED MUSHROOMS

Serve these spicy, piquant mushrooms well chilled, accompanied by lightly buttered wholewheat bread or crusty rolls.

Serves 4
Calories: 70 in each serving

450 g (1 lb) small white
   button mushrooms
2 tablespoons olive oil
2 teaspoons ground coriander
1 bay leaf

2 garlic cloves, peeled and
   crushed
Sea salt
2 tablespoons lemon juice
Freshly ground black pepper

To serve:
Crisp lettuce leaves, chopped
   fresh parsley

Wash the mushrooms, halving or quartering any larger ones, then fry them in the olive oil with the coriander, bay leaf and garlic for about 2 minutes, stirring all the time. Turn the mushrooms straight into a large bowl to prevent further cooking, then add the lemon juice and a grinding of black pepper. Cool then chill the mixture. Check the seasoning before serving the mushrooms piled up on lettuce leaves on individual plates.

TO FREEZE: unsuitable.

MELON WITH PORT

For this you need small melons so that everyone can have a half. The combination of the fragrant, sweet melon and the warming port is delicious.

Serves 4
Calories: about 120 for each serving

2 small ripe melons –
preferably charentais or
small cantaloupe, or ogen
or gallia

4 tablespoons sweet port

Cut the melons in half and scoop out the seeds. Put the melon halves on individual plates. Just before serving pour a spoonful of port into the centre of each melon half.

TO FREEZE: unsuitable.

PEARS WITH CREAMY TOPPING

Comice pears are perfect for this recipe if you can get them. They must be really ripe so that they slice easily with the spoon and melt in your mouth as you eat them.

Serves 4
Calories: 125 in each serving

2 tablespoons natural yoghurt
175 g (6 oz) curd cheese or
quark
1 tablespoon best quality
olive oil
2 teaspoons wine vinegar

$\frac{1}{2}$ teaspoon Dijon mustard
Sea salt and freshly ground
black pepper
2 ripe comice pears
8 lettuce leaves
A little paprika pepper

First make the topping: mix together the yoghurt, cheese, oil, wine vinegar and mustard; season with salt and pepper. Arrange a few lettuce leaves on four small serving dishes. Just before the meal, peel, halve and core the pears and arrange one half, core side down, on each dish. Spoon the topping over the pears, covering them completely, and sprinkle each with a little paprika.

TO FREEZE: unsuitable.

CREAMY TOMATOES WITH HORSERADISH

In this recipe sliced tomatoes are topped with a piquant creamy horseradish dressing.

Serves 6
Calories: 60 in each serving

6 large firm tomatoes
Sea salt and freshly ground
  black pepper
125 g (4 oz) curd cheese
2 tablespoons natural yoghurt

2 teaspoons olive oil
½ teaspoon wine vinegar
2 teaspoons horseradish sauce
Chopped fresh green herbs as
  available

Peel the tomatoes then slice them, cutting out any hard bits. Put the slices into six little dishes and season lightly with salt and pepper. To make the topping, put the curd cheese, yoghurt, oil, vinegar and horseradish sauce into a bowl and mix together until creamy. Season, then pour this mixture over the tomatoes and sprinkle with bright green herbs – chopped fresh basil, if you have it, otherwise chives, parsley or mint.

TO FREEZE: unsuitable.

STUFFED TOMATOES

This is another good way to serve firm, fragrant summer tomatoes. I think they're best with the skins removed, although I do sometimes leave them on if the tomatoes are very fresh and perfect.

Serves 4
Calories: 65 in each serving

4 medium-sized tomatoes
Sea salt
125 g (4 oz) quark

4 black olives
A few leaves of lettuce and
  sprigs of watercress

Skin the tomatoes, or just wash them and remove the stalks, whichever you prefer. Halve the tomatoes widthwise, scoop out the centres (these will not be needed for this recipe). Sprinkle the inside of each tomato with a little salt. Mix the quark with a fork, just to break it up a little, then spoon or pipe it into the tomato halves. Halve the olives, removing the stones. Top each tomato half with a piece of olive. Arrange the tomato halves on lettuce leaves on individual plates and garnish with a sprig or two of watercress.

TO FREEZE: unsuitable.

Salads

A well-made salad can be a mouthwatering mixture of contrasting colours, flavours and textures. I love making salads because of the scope they offer for exciting and imaginative combinations of different ingredients.

Although a certain amount of chopping and grating is usually involved, I do not think that a salad meal is as much trouble as a cooked meal. If you do make salads regularly, though, an electric grater and shredder does save time and effort. The other piece of equipment that I personally find indispensable when making salads, apart from a good chopping board and a sharp knife, is one of those circular spring-loaded choppers that you place over the food and bang up and down with your hand. I think this chops cabbage better than any other method.

Some people feel that a cooked meal is more nourishing than a cold one, but this is not so. In fact the reverse can be the case. Do watch, though, that you do not spoil it all by dressing the salad in too much oil. I certainly don't mean cut it out altogether, but just keep an eye on the amount you are using: for more ideas see the sauces and salad dressing section.

AVOCADO SALAD

In this recipe, as avocados form the main part of the salad, they do not seem too much of an extravagance economically or in terms of the amount of your day's fat 'ration' that they take. And they're so delicious with their creamy, nutty filling and glossy topping of well-flavoured dressing. Serve this salad with warm wholewheat rolls and follow with fresh fruit or a fruity pudding.

Serves 4

Calories: 575 in each serving. (If you're slimming you can reduce the calories by using cottage cheese and leaving out the walnuts and the dressing, in which case there are 415 calories.)

2 ripe avocados – they should feel pleasantly soft all over when held in the palm of your hand

Juice of half a lemon and a little of the grated rind

225 g (8 oz) curd cheese

1 garlic clove, peeled and crushed

50 g (2 oz) roughly chopped walnuts

Sea salt and freshly ground black pepper

Crisp leaves from half a medium-sized lettuce

4 tomatoes, sliced

4 medium-sized carrots, peeled, grated and mixed with a little lemon or orange juice

½ cucumber, coarsely grated

Half a bunch watercress

2 tablespoons good quality olive oil

1 tablespoon red wine vinegar

Cut the avocados in half, twist the halves apart and remove the stones. Brush the cut surfaces of the avocados with a little of the lemon juice.

Next make the filling for the avocados. Put the cheese into a bowl and stir in the remaining lemon juice, the garlic and enough of the grated lemon rind to give a pleasant tang. Mix in the walnuts and season the mixture with salt and freshly ground black pepper. Fill the avocado cavities with the mixture, piling it up well.

Line one large dish or four individual ones with the lettuce leaves. Put the avocados on top and arrange the sliced tomato, grated carrot, cucumber and watercress around them in colourful heaps. Mix together the oil and vinegar and season very well with salt and pepper. Spoon this over the top of the avocados just before serving.

If you want to you can make the filling for the avocados in advance but I think it's best not to add the walnuts until just before serving so that they stay crisp. Don't halve the avocados until the last minute, or they might discolour.

TO FREEZE: unsuitable.

CREAMY BUTTER BEAN AND AVOCADO SALAD

I had a delicious curried egg mayonnaise at a friend's house and I wanted to make something similar using a low-fat mayonnaise and something other than eggs, as my family aren't too keen on them. I decided on butter beans to replace the eggs, with avocados to give some richness, and although the result is certainly rather different from the original, it's creamy and delicious. You can serve this salad on a base of crisp lettuce or, if you want to make it more substantial, cold cooked rice.

Serves 4
Calories: 365 in each serving

100 g (3–4 oz) butter beans, soaked, cooked and drained, or a 425 g (15 oz) can, drained

1 large ripe avocado
Lemon juice

For the dressing:

1 tablespoon sunflower or corn oil

1 small onion, peeled and chopped

2 teaspoons curry powder

1 teaspoon tomato paste

6 tablespoons wine – red or white

1 teaspoon clear honey

150 g (5 oz) natural yoghurt

150 g (5 oz) fromage blanc

Sea salt and freshly ground black pepper

To serve:
Crisp lettuce or cold cooked rice, paprika pepper, sprigs of watercress

Put the beans into a large bowl. Cut the avocado in half, twist the two halves in opposite directions to separate and remove stone. Peel the avocado and cut the flesh into chunky dice. Sprinkle the avocado with lemon juice and add to the bowl with the beans.

To make the sauce, heat the oil in a medium-sized saucepan and fry the onion for 10 minutes, until it is soft but not brown. Stir in the curry powder, tomato paste, wine and honey and bubble

67

over a high heat for 2 or 3 minutes until reduced to a thick syrup. Cool. Put the yoghurt and fromage into a bowl and sieve in the onion mixture – or liquidize them all together. Season with salt and pepper.

Pour the yoghurt mixture over the beans and avocado and mix gently. Serve on a bed of lettuce or rice, sprinkled with a little paprika pepper and decorated with sprigs of watercress.

TO FREEZE: unsuitable.

CHICK PEA AND VEGETABLE MAYONNAISE

I love this French salad, but with its creamy mayonnaise dressing it's too high in fat and calories to enjoy very often. So I've gradually evolved ways of reducing the calories. Even slimmers can enjoy this latest version, yet I think you'll agree it's still very luxurious-tasting. It's lovely with warm wholewheat rolls. I must say I do love artichoke hearts, but if you don't approve of using tinned ones, use 225 g (8 oz) very fresh button mushrooms, just washed and sliced, instead.

Serves 4–6
Calories: 245 a portion if serving 4; 165 if serving 6

125 g (4 oz) chick peas, soaked overnight in cold water then rinsed and simmered in plenty of water until tender; or a 425 g (15 oz) can
350 g (12 oz) each of cooked carrots and cooked cut green beans
400 g (14 oz) can artichoke hearts, drained

150 ml ($\frac{1}{4}$ pint) natural yoghurt
125 g (4 oz) fromage blanc
2 large garlic cloves, peeled and crushed
1 tablespoon mayonnaise
1 tablespoon wine vinegar
Sea salt and freshly ground black pepper

To serve:
Crisp lettuce and watercress, chopped fresh parsley

68

Drain the chick peas and put them into a large bowl with the carrots and beans. Drain and quarter the artichoke hearts and add them to the bowl. To make the dressing, put the yoghurt, fromage blanc, garlic, mayonnaise and vinegar into a small bowl and mix well together until creamy. Season with salt and pepper. Pour the dressing over the vegetables and mix carefully until everything is well covered. Line a serving dish with lettuce and watercress, spoon the vegetable mixture on top and sprinkle with chopped parsley.

TO FREEZE: unsuitable.

CREAM CHEESE AND PINEAPPLE

When this salad is made with real cream cheese and syrupy canned pineapple it isn't particularly good for you. But if instead you use low-fat quark, which tastes beautifully creamy, and pineapple rings which have been canned in their own juice, it's light, healthy and, I think, very delicious.

Serves 4
Calories: 160 in each serving

Crisp leaves from 1 small
  lettuce
Half a bunch of watercress
227 g (8 oz) can pineapple
  rings in their own juice
250 g (8¾ oz) low-fat quark

2 carrots, scraped and grated
4 tomatoes, sliced
Half a cucumber, coarsely
  grated
A few radishes when available

Cover the base of one large dish or four small ones with the lettuce and watercress. Drain the pineapple, reserving the juice, and put the rings on top of the lettuce. Place a mound of quark on top of each of the rings, dividing it between them. Moisten the grated carrot with the reserved juice. Spoon little heaps of this carrot mixture on the plate or plates and also the sliced tomatoes, cucumber and radishes.

TO FREEZE: unsuitable.

FRUIT SALAD WITH CREAMY TOPPING
AND ALMONDS

I think this is a luscious salad: fresh juicy fruits under a creamy, slightly sharp-tasting dressing, topped with crunchy golden almonds. Serve it with warm home-made scones if you want to make it more substantial.

Serves 4
Calories: 300 in each serving, or 210 without almonds

3 sweet dessert apples
2 pears
3 large oranges
225 g (8 oz) grapes – or strawberries when in season
2 peaches, if available, or a wedge of melon

225 g (8 oz) fromage blanc
4 tablespoons liquid skimmed milk
A few crisp lettuce leaves
50 g (2 oz) flaked almonds, toasted golden under the grill
Sprigs of fresh watercress

Wash the apples and pears thoroughly to remove any residues of sprays etc.; remove skin if you think it's necessary. Cut them into even-sized pieces, removing the cores. Put the pieces into a large bowl and hold the oranges over the bowl as you cut away the pith and peel, so that you catch all the juice. Cut the orange segments away from the white skin and add them to the bowl. Squeeze the remains of the oranges over the bowl to extract any extra juice. Wash, halve and de-seed the grapes or hull and halve the strawberries. If you're using peaches, halve them, remove stones and cut the flesh into pieces; or cut up melon flesh, discarding skin. Mix all the prepared fruits together in the bowl.

To make the topping, put the fromage blanc into a bowl and stir in the skimmed milk to make a smooth, fairly thick consistency.

Line a serving dish with lettuce leaves, spoon on the fruit mixture, then cover with the creamy dressing, so that just a few pieces of fruit peep out at the sides. Scatter the flaked almonds on top and push a few sprigs of watercress round the edges.

TO FREEZE: unsuitable.

HAZEL NUT AND CREAM CHEESE
SALAD LOAF

This is an unusual dish, a loaf of creamy low-fat white cheese and hazel nuts flavoured with the tang of lemon and coated with crisp breadcrumbs. People usually start by wondering what it is and end by asking for the recipe! I invented it one day when I was feeling rather lazy and didn't want to cook, so it's easy to make and keeps well in either the fridge or the freezer. Serve it with lots of fresh salad.

Serves 4–6
Calories: 250 a portion if serving 4; 170 a portion if serving 6

250 g (8¾ oz) low-fat quark
125 g (4 oz) hazel nuts roasted on a dry baking sheet in a moderate oven until golden then grated – the liquidizer is good for this

Juice and grated rind of ½ small lemon
2 tablespoons chopped parsley
Sea salt, freshly ground black pepper, paprika pepper
50 g (2 oz) crisp wholewheat breadcrumbs

To serve:
Crisp lettuce, tomatoes, cucumber, grated carrot,
sprigs of watercress as desired

Put the quark, hazel nuts, lemon juice and rind and parsley into a bowl and mix until well combined. Add salt and pepper to taste and one or two pinches of paprika pepper. Have ready a square of greaseproof paper or foil sprinkled with dried crumbs. Turn the cream cheese mixture on to this; form it into a loaf shape, making sure that it is completely coated with the crumbs. You can use the paper to help you to form the roll shape. Then wrap the roll up in the paper and put into the fridge to chill for several hours. It firms up as it chills. To serve, place the roll on a bed of crisp, dry lettuce and surround with sliced tomato, cucumber, grated carrot, watercress and anything else you fancy.

TO FREEZE: the cream cheese roll freezes well. Open-freeze then wrap well when solid. To use, remove wrapping, place roll on a plate and leave until defrosted.

HEALTHY PLOUGHMAN'S LUNCH

A traditional ploughman's lunch of crusty bread, cheese and pickles makes a delicious meal. It can be a very healthy one, too, if you use wholewheat bread and include some salad. Spreading the bread with mild mustard cuts down on the fat and calories, but you could of course use a little butter or margarine if you prefer.

Serves 4
Calories: 390 in each serving

450 g (1 lb) wholewheat loaf – one of those oval ones from the supermarket is best if you can get it
2 tablespoons mild French mustard
225 g (8 oz) Edam or Cheshire cheese

4 large tomatoes
1 medium-sized onion, peeled
8 pickled gherkins
Sea salt and freshly ground black pepper

To serve:
Bowl of crisp green salad, fingers of carrot, celery sticks

Slice the bread in half lengthwise and scoop out a little of the crumb to make room for the filling. Spread the cut sides of the bread with mustard. If you're using Edam cheese, trim off the rind. Slice the cheese thinly and arrange the slices on one of the pieces of bread. Thinly slice the tomatoes, onions and gherkins and put them on top of the cheese. Sprinkle lightly with salt and pepper, then place the other piece of bread on top, pressing down firmly to hold the filling in place. Using a sharp knife, cut the loaf into four or eight pieces. Serve with the salad and cider, beer, lager or sparkling apple juice.

TO FREEZE: unsuitable when assembled, but the loaves keep well in the freezer.

MEXICAN SALAD

In Mexico this salad might be served on top of unleavened bread, a taco or crisp tortilla. We like it best just as it is, but you can make it more substantial by putting everything on top of a large slice of wholewheat bread rather like an open sandwich that you eat with a knife and fork. It's a particularly pleasant blend of flavours and textures and the avocado topping gives the final touch.

Serves 4
Calories: about 375 in each serving

100 g (3–4 oz) red kidney beans soaked and cooked, or use a 425 g (15 oz) can
1 large ripe avocado
1 garlic clove, peeled and crushed
1 tablespoon olive oil
1 teaspoon wine vinegar
Sea salt, freshly ground black pepper, chilli powder
8 large crisp lettuce leaves
1 small onion, peeled and thinly sliced
4 firm tomatoes, sliced
1 small green or red pepper, de-seeded and thinly sliced
125 g (4 oz) grated cheese or 4 hardboiled eggs, sliced
Paprika pepper

Drain the beans. Halve the avocado, remove stone and skin. Put the avocado into a medium-sized bowl and mash with a fork. Add the garlic, oil and vinegar to the avocado, also a seasoning of salt and pepper and a pinch of chilli powder. Mix well to a creamy consistency.

Place two lettuce leaves on each plate. Spoon the beans over the lettuce and top with layers of onion, tomato, pepper and cheese or egg. Finish with a big dollop of the avocado cream and a good sprinkling of bright red paprika pepper. Serve as soon as possible.

TO FREEZE: unsuitable.

SALADE NICOISE

This is a pretty salad: tomato, hardboiled egg, French beans and plump black olives glistening with dressing. If you don't like eggs you could use drained butter beans (100 g [3–4 oz] dry weight or a 425 g (15 oz) can), or 125 g (4 oz) roasted cashew nuts. Serve the salad with warm crunchy wholewheat rolls.

Serves 4
Calories: 235 in each serving (same calories if using beans instead of eggs, but 315 calories with nuts)

1 large lettuce
1 medium-sized onion, peeled
450 g (1 lb) firm tomatoes
5 hardboiled eggs
450 g (1 lb) cooked French
   beans
12 black olives

2 tablespoons chopped fresh
   parsley
2 tablespoons best quality
   olive oil
1 tablespoon red wine vinegar
Sea salt and freshly ground
   black pepper

Line a flat serving dish with the lettuce. Thinly slice the onion, quarter the tomatoes and eggs, cut the French beans into even-sized lengths. Put the vegetables and eggs into a bowl and add the olives, parsley, oil and vinegar and a little salt and pepper. Mix gently so that everything gets coated with the dressing and looks glossy and appetising. Heap the salad up on top of the lettuce and serve as soon as possible.

TO FREEZE: unsuitable.

SPECIAL RICE SALAD

I find rice salads very useful for busy weekends because they can be made in advance and kept for a couple of days or so in the fridge or in the freezer. This is a well-flavoured rice salad and the crunchy golden cashew nuts make it extra good, although you could leave them out if you're slimming, or reduce the calories to 380 a helping by using hazel nuts instead. Served with some lettuce and watercress, or a mixed green salad, this makes a complete main course.

Serves 4
Calories: 450 in each serving, or 275 without the nuts

1 medium-sized aubergine
Sea salt
225 g (8 oz) long grain brown rice
400 ml (¾ pint) water
2 onions, peeled and chopped
3–4 garlic cloves, peeled and crushed
1 tablespoon sunflower oil
1 red pepper
225 g (8 oz) button mushrooms, washed
4 tomatoes, peeled and chopped
1 tablespoon wine vinegar
Tabasco sauce, freshly ground black pepper
125 g (4 oz) cashew nuts, roasted on a dry baking sheet in a moderate oven until golden

Wash the aubergine and remove stalk. Cut the flesh into dice, sprinkle with salt and leave on one side for the bitter juices to be drawn out. Put the rice and water into a saucepan with 1 teaspoonful of salt; bring to the boil, then cover and leave to cook over a very gentle heat for 45 minutes. The rice should be tender but still have a little bite to it.

While the rice is cooking, fry the onion and garlic in the oil for 10 minutes, until softened. Halve, de-seed and chop the pepper and add to the onions. Squeeze the aubergines, then rinse them under cold water and pat them dry; add to the onion mixture. Cook for 5–10 minutes, until the aubergine and pepper are almost tender, then add the mushrooms and fry for a further 2 minutes, just to cook the mushrooms briefly. Stir in the tomatoes, then remove from the heat.

When the rice is cooked, turn it into a large bowl and add the vegetables, mixing lightly with a fork. Stir in the wine vinegar, a few drops of tabasco, a good grinding of pepper and a little more salt if necessary. Cool. Stir in the cashew nuts just before serving.

TO FREEZE: don't add the nuts if you're going to freeze the salad:

they can be roasted and kept in an airtight jar or tin to add later. To use the salad, allow plenty of time for it to de-freeze – it's best to take it out of the freezer the night before if you can remember, but in any case it takes at least 3 hours.

SERVE-YOURSELF-SALAD

This is my version of the salad they serve at one of our favourite local eating places, Clinch's, in Chichester. The salad consists of lots of bowls of different ingredients, chosen to contrast as much as possible in colour, flavour and texture. When I serve it at home everyone makes their own selection, ending with a dollop of one of the lovely low-fat creamy dressings. It's quite a labour-saving salad to make if you cook the wheat and beans in batches – I do a 500 g (1·1 lb) bag at a time, divide the beans into five boxes and store them in the freezer.

Serves 4–6
Calories: about 425 if serving 4, 280 if serving 6 (without jacket potato); 1 tablespoon low-calorie mayonnaise 35 extra

100 g (3–4 oz) red kidney beans
100 g (3–4 oz) whole grain wheat – from health shops
2 tablespoons olive oil
2 tablespoons red wine vinegar
Sea salt and freshly ground black pepper
1 teaspoon tomato paste
A dash of honey
Potato salad, made as described on page 132

To serve:
Jacket baked potatoes

1 small-medium lettuce, washed and shredded
3 carrots, peeled, grated and tossed in a little orange juice
2 raw beetroots, peeled, grated and tossed in a little orange juice
4 tomatoes, sliced
1 punnet of mustard and cress, cut and washed
½ cucumber, diced
Low-calorie mayonnaise, page 120

Put the beans and wheat into separate bowls and soak them over-

76

night in cold water. Next day drain and rinse the beans and wheat and cook them in plenty of water until tender: 1 hour for the beans (20 minutes in a pressure-cooker), 1¼ hours for the wheat (25 minutes in a pressure-cooker). Drain them both. Mix half the oil and vinegar with the beans and half with the wheat. Season both mixtures with salt and pepper and add a dash of tomato paste and just a very little honey to the beans. Leave to cool. Serve all the other ingredients separately in little bowls – soup bowls, or small wooden bowls if you have them.

TO FREEZE: the red bean mixture and the wheat both freeze well; put them into small polythene bags or small containers. Thaw, then use.

THREE-BEAN SALAD WITH MUSTARD DRESSING

There are many versions of this popular salad and the best ones are made from beans which contrast well in colour, flavour and shape. I like to use green French beans as a basis because they are low in calories as well as having a lovely fresh flavour. In this recipe they're mixed with broad beans and red kidney beans and tossed in a tangy mustard dressing. To make a main course of this salad, serve it with warm wholewheat bread or rolls, or crunchy jacket potatoes and a bowl of fresh salad – carrot, apple, celery and raisin salad goes well with it.

Serves 4
Calories: 200 in each serving

100 g (3–4 oz) red kidney beans, soaked and cooked, or use a 425 g (15 oz) can
225 g (8 oz) frozen broad beans
225 g (8 oz) French beans, frozen, or fresh ones, trimmed
Sea salt

1 tablespoon mild mustard – a whole-grain type is good
3 tablespoons olive oil
1 tablespoon wine vinegar
Freshly ground black pepper, summer savory
Fresh chopped parsley

Drain the red kidney beans and put them into a large bowl. Cook the broad beans and the French beans in a little fast-boiling lightly salted water until just tender. They can be done in the same saucepan, but if the French beans are fresh and very thin and tender, add them after the others have been cooking for 4 minutes, then cook for a further 3 minutes. Drain the beans and add them to the bowl with the red kidney beans. Next mix up the dressing. Put the mustard into a small bowl and stir in the oil, vinegar, some salt and pepper and a pinch or two of summer savory if you have it. Mix well, then pour into the bowl with the beans. Turn the beans with a spoon so that they all get covered with the dressing. If possible let the salad stand for half an hour or so, to let the flavours blend. Spoon the salad into a serving dish – a glass one looks good – and sprinkle with chopped parsley.

TO FREEZE: rather than try to freeze the completed salad, it's best just to keep the individual packets of frozen beans in the freezer ready to make the salad up when required – it's very quick to assemble.

Vegetables

AUBERGINES WITH MUSHROOM AND PARSLEY STUFFING

Aubergines are useful because they're bulky without being calorific and have a light texture and a delicious, subtle flavour. Instead of salting and frying the aubergines in the usual way you will see that I reduce the fat in the recipe by par-boiling them whole, first, then halving and stuffing them. I find this works very well and haven't had any problems with bitterness.

Serves 6
Calories: 170 in each serving

3 medium-sized aubergines
2 onions, peeled and chopped
1 tablespoon oil
350 g (12 oz) button
  mushrooms, washed and
  chopped

2 tablespoons chopped parsley
175 g (6 oz) low-fat quark
125 g (4 oz) grated cheese
Sea salt and freshly ground
  black pepper
1 tomato, cut into 6 slices

Wipe the aubergines and remove the leafy stalk ends. Half fill a large saucepan with water and bring to the boil. Put in the aubergines and let them simmer for 15–20 minutes, until they feel tender when pierced with the point of a knife. Cool. Cut the aubergines in half and carefully scoop out as much of the inside as you can, leaving just a shell of skin to hold the stuffing.

Set the oven to 200°C (400°F), gas mark 6. Fry the onion in the oil for 10 minutes, then add the chopped mushrooms and cook for a further 2–3 minutes. Remove from the heat and stir in the parsley, quark, grated cheese, aubergine flesh and salt and pepper to taste.

Put the aubergine skins on a lightly-greased shallow ovenproof

79

dish and divide the filling between them, piling it up well. Place a slice of tomato on top of each stuffed aubergine. Bake for about 45 minutes. I like these aubergines with a vegetable purée, such as potato and celeriac or carrot and lemon, and whole French beans or mange tout peas. If you want to introduce a crisp texture, crunchy roast potatoes are good with them or some triangles of crisp wholewheat toast.

TO FREEZE: unsuitable.

STUFFED AUBERGINES IN TOMATO AND WINE SAUCE

Although this is a very healthy dish, being low in calories and fat, it is always popular and one which I think is suitable for a special occasion.

Serves 6
Calories: 240 in each serving

3 medium-sized aubergines
1 tablespoon vegetable oil
4 onions, peeled and chopped
3 large garlic cloves, peeled and crushed
1 green pepper, de-seeded and chopped
3 tablespoons tomato paste
8 tablespoons red wine
125 g (4 oz) very finely grated cashew nuts

1 heaped tablespoon finely chopped parsley
Pinch each of marjoram, thyme and rosemary
Salt and freshly ground black pepper
A little honey – about 1 teaspoon or less
2 425 g (15 oz) cans tomatoes

Par-boil the aubergines whole as in the previous recipe. Cool, halve and scoop out the flesh. Place the skins in a lightly greased shallow ovenproof dish. Heat the oil in a fairly large saucepan and fry the onions for 10 minutes. Remove half the onion and put it straight into your liquidizer goblet – this is for the sauce, leave it on one side for a moment.

Add the garlic, green pepper and scooped-out aubergine pulp to the rest of the onion in the saucepan, also two tablespoons of the tomato paste, 4 tablespoons of the wine and the nuts and herbs. Season with salt and pepper and add a very little honey if you think necessary – this just seems to 'lift' the flavour without tasting at all sweet. Pile the mixture into the aubergine skins.

Finish making the sauce: add the tomatoes to the onion in the liquidizer, together with the remaining wine and tomato paste, a seasoning of salt and pepper and a little dash of honey. Blend until fairly smooth, then check seasoning, adding salt, pepper and a little honey as necessary and pour about half the sauce around the aubergines in the dish. Bake at 180°C (350°F), gas mark 4, for 1 hour. Serve the aubergines from the dish and hand round the remaining sauce separately. Very light mashed potato and a cooked green vegetable go well with this dish.

TO FREEZE: unsuitable.

AUBERGINE AND TOMATO CASSEROLE

This is a useful dish because it's very quick to prepare and adaptable. It's delicious with hot crusty wholewheat rolls, Bircher potatoes, brown rice or wholewheat spaghetti which has been tossed in a little olive oil and flavoured with freshly ground black pepper. The potatoes and the rice can be baked in the oven with the casserole. Serve with some grated cheese or roasted nuts or sunflower seeds, which can be forked into the brown rice, if you're having that. A crisp salad is good with it, and, for a special occasion, try adding a glassful of wine.

Serves 4
Calories: 85 in each serving, about 100 with wine

2 large aubergines – about 450 g (1 lb)	142 g (5 oz) can tomato paste
2 large onions, peeled and sliced	225 g (8 oz) baby mushrooms
397 g (14 oz) can tomatoes	Salt and freshly ground black pepper, a little honey

Set the oven to 180°C (350°F), gas mark 4. Wash the aubergines, remove the stalks. Cut the aubergines into very thin rounds, put into a bowl, cover with boiling water. Leave for 5 minutes, then drain. Put everything (and the wine if you're using it) into an ovenproof dish and mix lightly. Cover and bake for $1\frac{1}{2}$ hours.

TO FREEZE: unsuitable.

CHINESE VEGETABLES WITH ALMONDS

A Chinese-style vegetable dish is pleasant for a change and, served with some brown rice, makes a surprisingly substantial main dish. If you get all the basic preparation done in advance, the actual cooking takes only a few minutes, just before you want to serve the meal. Some tinned pineapple pieces – the kind canned in their own juice – are also good added to this mixture if you like a touch of sweetness.

Serves 4
Calories: 320 in each serving

450 g (1 lb) white salad cabbage, finely shredded
1 large onion, peeled and finely sliced
1 large carrot, scraped and finely diced
1 turnip, peeled and finely diced
225 g (8 oz) button mushrooms, washed and sliced
300 g (10 oz) bean sprouts, washed
1 garlic clove, peeled and crushed

2 tablespoons arrowroot or cornflour
1 tablespoon soy sauce
2 teaspoons clear honey
4 tablespoons cheap sherry
1–2 teaspoons salt
1 tablespoon sunflower or corn oil
Salt and freshly ground black pepper
125 g (4 oz) flaked almonds, toasted under a moderate grill until crisp and golden

Have all the vegetables prepared ready to cook. Put the cornflour or arrowroot into a small bowl or cup and mix to a smooth paste with the soy sauce, honey, sherry and salt. Heat the oil in a large saucepan (or a wok, if you have one) and add the cabbage, onion, carrot and turnip. Fry, stirring often, for 3 minutes, then

82

add the rest of the vegetables, including the garlic, and fry for a further 1–2 minutes. Give the sherry mixture a quick stir, then pour it in with the vegetables, stirring for a moment or two until thickened. Add the almonds then serve immediately, with the rice.

TO FREEZE: unsuitable.

COTTAGE CHEESE AND SPINACH BAKE

Cottage cheese mixed with vegetables and baked in the oven makes a pleasant light bake that's good for lunch or as a slimmer's savoury. The flaked almond topping adds a lovely crunchy contrasting texture but could of course be left off if you want to save a few extra calories.

Serves 2
Calories: 245 in each serving or 200 without the almonds

10 oz packet frozen spinach, thawed, or 450 g (1 lb) fresh, washed, chopped, cooked and drained.
225 g (8 oz) cottage cheese
2 teaspoons mild whole seed mustard

Sea salt and freshly ground black pepper
1 tablespoon finely grated Parmesan cheese
15 g ($\frac{1}{2}$ oz) flaked almonds, toasted under a moderate grill

Set the oven to 190°C (350°F), gas mark 5. Mix together the spinach, cottage cheese and mustard. Season with salt and pepper. Spoon into a small shallow ovenproof dish and sprinkle the Parmesan cheese over the top. Bake for 30 minutes. Sprinkle with the almonds if you're using them and serve with a crunchy salad, such as the celery and apple salad, or with grilled tomatoes and green beans.

TO FREEZE: unsuitable.

GREEN PEPPER AND TOMATO BAKE

This is an economical family bake that's quick to make and low in calories. I like it best with a tomato sauce and Bircher potatoes – see sections on sauces and vegetables – and cauliflower or a lightly-cooked green vegetable.

Serves 4
Calories: 290 in each portion

1 large onion, peeled and chopped
1 small/medium green pepper, de-seeded and chopped
225 g (8 oz) can tomatoes
125 g (4 oz) wholewheat bread

175 g (6 oz) grated cheese
2 tablespoons chopped parsley
1 egg
½–1 teaspoon tabasco sauce
Sea salt and freshly ground black pepper

Set the oven to 200°C (400°F), gas mark 6. Put the onion, pepper and tomatoes into a bowl and crumble in the bread with your fingers. Mix well to break up the bread. Add most of the grated cheese, the parsley, the beaten egg and enough tabasco sauce to give a pleasant 'lift'. Season with salt and pepper. Spoon mixture into a shallow, lightly-greased ovenproof dish, sprinkle with the remaining cheese and bake for 40–50 minutes, until set and golden brown.

TO FREEZE: this dish freezes well, either fully cooked or par-baked.

MUSHROOM LOAF

This tasty loaf is good either hot or cold. It slices well when cold and can be used as a sandwich filling.

Serves 6

Calories: 270 in each serving if using Brazil or cashew nuts; 250–260 with the other nuts

450 g (1 lb) mushrooms
1 onion
1 tablespoon sunflower oil
2 tablespoons skimmed milk
  powder
125 g (4 oz) grated nuts –
  Brazils or cashews, or
  ground almonds if you're in
  a hurry

225 g (8 oz) soft wholewheat
  breadcrumbs
1 teaspoon Marmite
1 teaspoon mixed herbs
1 egg
Salt and freshly ground black
  pepper
Dried crumbs to
  coat tin

Set the oven to 180°C (350°F), gas mark 4. Wash the mushrooms and chop them roughly. Peel and chop the onion. Fry the onion in the oil in a large saucepan for 7 minutes, then add the mushrooms and fry for a further 3 minutes. Remove from the heat and liquidize. Add all the remaining ingredients and season to taste. Grease a 450 g (1 lb) loaf tin generously with butter or soft margarine and coat well with dried crumbs. Spoon the mushroom mixture into this and smooth the top. Bake, uncovered, for 1 hour. Slip a knife round the sides of the tin and turn the loaf out. Serve in slices, with a savoury sauce and vegetables.

TO FREEZE: this loaf freezes beautifully. Cook it as described, remove from tin, cool and open-freeze. Wrap in polythene. To use, remove wrappings and place the loaf either in a loaf tin or on a baking sheet. When thawed, bake in a moderate oven for about 40 minutes, until heated through.

POTATO BAKE

Potatoes are an undervalued food. Yet they're cheap, popular and very nutritious, containing useful amounts of iron, vitamin C and protein, as well as fibre. I like dishes which make potatoes into a main meal. This bake makes a simple, homely supper that children love. It's good with a tomato sauce and a green vegetable. You can leave the skins on the potatoes, but I think it's better if they're peeled.

Serves 4
Calories: 260 in each serving

450 g (1 lb) potatoes, peeled
15 g ($\frac{1}{2}$ oz) vegetable
  margarine
1 garlic clove, crushed

Sea salt and freshly ground
  black pepper
125 g (4 oz) grated cheese
4 tablespoons milk

Set oven to 160°C (325°F), gas mark 3. Slice the potatoes finely – this is quickly done with the slicing side of a grater. Mix the margarine and garlic and use half to grease a shallow ovenproof dish. Put a layer of potatoes in the base of the dish, sprinkle with salt, pepper and some of the cheese. Continue like this until everything is in, ending with potatoes. Pour the milk over the top, dot with the remaining margarine. Bake for 1$\frac{1}{2}$ hours, until the potato is tender.

TO FREEZE: unsuitable.

POTATO CAKES

Potato cakes can be delicious, creamy on the inside, crisp on the outside. If you add a little protein, in the form of grated cheese, chopped nuts or sunflower seeds, they make a good main dish and are very popular with children.

Serves 4
Calories: 340 in each serving (2 cakes) if using cheese, 330–400 if using nuts or seeds

450 g (1 lb) potatoes
About 150 ml ($\frac{1}{4}$ pint)
  skimmed milk
125 g (4 oz) grated cheese,
  nuts (any type) or
  sunflower seeds
2 tablespoons chopped
  parsley

Salt and freshly ground black
  pepper
50 g (2 oz) wholewheat flour
  to coat
2 tablespoons oil

Scrub the potatoes, cover with water and boil until tender. Drain, cool slightly, then slip off the skins with a small sharp knife. Mash, adding enough skimmed milk to make a firm consistency. Stir in the cheese, nuts or sunflower seeds, the parsley and seasoning. Add some more milk if necessary – the mixture must be manageable but not too dry. Divide into eight pieces, coat in flour and fry in the oil until crisp on both sides. Drain and serve as soon as possible with salad or with a sauce and cooked vegetables.

TO FREEZE: unsuitable.

VEGETABLE CASSEROLE

You can use all kinds of vegetables for this casserole, as available. It's good served just as it is, or with an extra cooked green vegetable such as sprouts, and grated cheese or roasted nuts for protein if you wish.

Serves 4
Calories: 225 in each serving

1 tablespoon oil
3 onions, peeled and sliced
450 g (1 lb) carrots, scraped and sliced
450 g (1 lb) potatoes, peeled and cut into even-sized pieces
2 sticks of celery, washed and sliced
125–225 g (4–8 oz) button

mushrooms, wiped and sliced
2 tablespoons flour
575 ml (1 pint) water
2 vegetable stock cubes
1 tablespoon tomato paste
2 bay leaves
Sea salt, freshly milled black pepper and perhaps a dash of honey

Set oven to 190°C (375°F), gas mark 5. Heat the oil in a large saucepan and fry the onions for 5 minutes. Add the rest of the vegetables and fry for a further couple of minutes, stirring often. Then mix in the flour; when it is well distributed add the water, stock cubes, tomato paste, bay leaves and a little salt and pepper – you won't need much because of the stock cubes. Bring mixture up to the boil, then transfer to a heatproof casserole and bake for

1 hour. Check the seasoning and add a very little honey if you think it needs it.

TO FREEZE: unsuitable.

Pulses

Pulses are very useful from the health point of view because they're such a good source of fibre. They are also low in fat and very nutritious. And they can be very good to eat, too, when combined with other tasty ingredients.

Some of the pulses take an hour or so to cook even after an initial soaking, so when I cook red kidney beans, butter beans or chick peas I usually do 500 g (1·1 lb) at a time in the pressure-cooker, divide into five equal portions and store in old cottage cheese or margarine cartons, well labelled, in the freezer. This means there are always some handy when I need them and they really are very little bother.

Instead of soaking the beans overnight, I usually put them straight into the pressure-cooker, cover with cold water, bring to the boil, then leave them to stand for an hour. After that I drain and rinse them and cook them for 15 minutes in the pressure-cooker or 1–1½ hours normal simmering. For more details, see *The Bean Book*.

When you use red kidney beans do make sure that they come to the boil and then boil hard for 8–10 minutes before you turn the heat down, to destroy any harmful enzymes present. As long as you do this they are perfectly safe, and one of the tastiest of beans.

BUTTER BEANS AND MUSHROOMS IN CREAMY SAUCE

If you've been able to soak and cook the butter beans in advance or are willing to use a tin, this dish can be very quickly made. It's creamy and delicious, good with plainly cooked rice and a crisp green salad.

Serves 3
Calories: 200 in each serving; rice extra

1 tablespoon sunflower oil
1 large onion, peeled and
  chopped
225 g (8 oz) small white
  button mushrooms
100 g (4 oz) butter beans,
  soaked, rinsed and cooked
  for a good hour until
  tender – or a 425 g
  (15 oz) can

150 ml (6 oz) fromage blanc
½ teaspoon paprika pepper
Sea salt and freshly ground
  black pepper
Chopped parsley

Heat the oil in a medium-sized saucepan and fry the onion for about 7 minutes, until nearly soft but not brown. While the onion is frying, wash and slice the mushrooms, then add them to the saucepan with the butter beans and cook for about 5 minutes, until the mushrooms are tender and the butter beans heated through. Stir mixture often. Add the fromage blanc and bring just up to the boil, stirring all the time. Then take off the heat, add the paprika and some salt and pepper to taste and serve immediately, sprinkled with chopped parsley. The mixture mustn't get too hot after you've added the fromage blanc or it will curdle a little. It will still taste all right but it won't look as good.

TO FREEZE: unsuitable.

LENTIL BURGERS

These tasty lentil burgers are crisp on the outside and soft within. They're quite easy to make, cheap and popular with both children and adults. They're good served with a dollop of natural yoghurt or one of the low-fat mayonnaises, salad and wholewheat bread, or with a tasty sauce and cooked vegetables.

Serves 4
Calories: 300 in each serving (2 burgers)

90

225 g (8 oz) split red lentils
300 ml (½ pint) water
1 bay leaf
2 large onions, peeled and
finely chopped
1 tablespoon chopped parsley
1 tablespoon lemon juice

1 egg
Sea salt and freshly ground
black pepper
50–75 g (2–3 oz) fine fresh
wholewheat breadcrumbs
2 tablespoons oil for frying

Put the lentils, water and bay leaf into a medium-sized saucepan and cook very gently for 20 25 minutes, until the lentils are tender and pale gold in colour. Add the onions, parsley, lemon juice and egg, mashing the lentils as you do so and mixing to a fairly smooth, thick consistency. Season well with salt and pepper. Form mixture into eight burgers and coat each thoroughly in breadcrumbs, pressing to make them stick. Heat the oil in a frying pan and fry the burgers on both sides over a moderate heat until crisp. Drain well and serve as soon as possible.

TO FREEZE: these freeze very well and I usually make a double or triple quantity. Coat the burgers with breadcrumbs but don't fry them. Open-freeze them on a baking tin then pack them in a polythene bag when solid. They can be cooked from frozen.

LENTIL LOAF

A friend of mine has almost converted her meat-loving in-laws to vegetarianism with the aid of this loaf. It's good either hot or cold, and slices well, especially when cold. If you're serving it hot, a savoury sauce, Bircher or roast potatoes and a green vegetable go well with it. Chutney or one of the low-fat mayonnaises are pleasant accompaniments if you want to have the loaf cold. Slices of the cold loaf make an excellent open sandwich topped with the mayonnaise, circles of tomato and onion, and some chutney or pickles.

Serves 4–6
Calories: 360 if serving 4; 240 if serving 6

175 g (6 oz) split red lentils
225 g (8 fl oz) water
1 bay leaf
125 g (4 oz) grated cheese
1 medium-sized onion, peeled and finely chopped
50 g (2 oz) button mushrooms, washed and finely chopped
40 g (1½ oz) fine fresh whole-wheat breadcrumbs

1 tablespoon chopped parsley
1 tablespoon lemon juice
1 egg
Sea salt and freshly ground black pepper
Butter and dried crumbs for coating tin

Put the lentils, water and bay leaf into a medium-sized saucepan and simmer very gently, uncovered, until the lentils are tender and all the liquid absorbed – about 20 minutes. Remove bay leaf.

Set the oven to 190°C (375°F), gas mark 5. Prepare a 450 g (1 lb) loaf tin by putting a long narrow strip of bakewell paper on the base and up the narrow sides. Grease the tin well with butter or margarine – I find the loaf comes out of the tin best if I use butter – and sprinkle generously with dried crumbs.

Add the grated cheese, onion, mushrooms, breadcrumbs, chopped parsley, lemon juice and egg to the lentils, mixing well. Season with plenty of salt and pepper. Spoon the mixture into the tin and level the top. Bake, uncovered, for 45–60 minutes, until firm and golden-brown on top.

TO FREEZE: lentil loaf freezes very well and it's worth making a double batch if you like it. Cook or half cook the loaf, then open-freeze until firm. Wrap in polythene. To use, unwrap and put the loaf back into a lightly-greased tin. Bake in a moderate oven for about 40 minutes until heated through.

SPICED LENTILS WITH RICE

This is a deliciously spicy dish, very tasty and filling. It's good with just a side salad such as tomato and onion or cabbage and pine-apple. If there's any over it's also very nice cold as a protein salad, served in a border of watercress and sliced tomato, with warm wholewheat bread.

Serves 4
Calories: 185 in each serving

175 g (6 oz) brown lentils
700 ml (1¼ pints) water
1 bay leaf
1 tablespoon oil
1 onion, peeled and chopped
1 green or red pepper,
 de-seeded and sliced
1 garlic clove, peeled and
 crushed

175 g (6 oz) button mushrooms,
 washed
2 tomatoes, washed and sliced
1 teaspoon curry powder
1 teaspoon ground coriander
1 tablespoon lemon juice
1 tablespoon tomato paste
Sea salt and freshly ground
 pepper

Put the lentils, water and bay leaf into a medium-sized saucepan
and simmer gently for 45–60 minutes, until lentils are very tender.
Remove bay leaf. Heat the oil in a large saucepan and fry the
onion for 5 minutes, until beginning to soften, then add the
pepper, garlic, mushrooms, tomatoes and lentils and fry for a
further 2–3 minutes. Add the spices, lemon juice and tomato paste
and cook gently for a further 4–5 minutes, until everything is
heated through. Check seasoning and serve, garnished with the
raw onion rings and remaining tomato.

TO FREEZE: this freezes well. Cool mixture, then put into a rigid
container and freeze. To use, thaw completely, then heat gently,
either in the oven, or over a low heat, stirring frequently.

TASTY BROWN LENTIL LOAF WITH PINEAPPLE

This lentil loaf is different from the preceding one because it uses
those big brown continental lentils that you can get at health
shops. These stay intact when they're cooked, giving a pleasantly
chewy texture. The pineapple adds interest and gives just the right
touch of sweetness.

Serves 4
Calories: 220 in each serving

150 g (5 oz) continental lentils
2 large onions, peeled and
finely chopped
2 tablespoons chopped parsley
1 teaspoon mixed herbs
1 teaspoon Marmite
1 tablespoon lemon juice

75 g (3 oz) soft wholewheat
breadcrumbs
Sea salt and freshly ground
black pepper
1 tablespoon oil
225 g (8 oz) can pineapple rings
in juice

Put the lentils into a medium-sized saucepan and cover with plenty of water. Simmer gently for about 45 minutes, until lentils are soft. Drain. Set the oven to 200°C (400°F), gas mark 6. Add the onion, parsley, herbs, Marmite, lemon juice and two-thirds of the crumbs to the lentils and mix well. The mixture should be firm enough to hold its shape – add a few more crumbs if necessary. Season with salt and pepper. Form lentil mixture into a loaf shape and coat with the remaining crumbs. Brush a baking tin with the oil and lift the loaf on to the tin, using a fish slice to help if needed. Bake for 40–45 minutes, turning the loaf over, again with the aid of a fish slice, after about 30 minutes. Put the pineapple, together with its juice, into a small heatproof container and place in the oven to heat through about 15 minutes before the loaf is ready. Serve the lentil loaf in slices, with the pineapple, a tasty sauce, potatoes and a lightly-cooked green vegetable.

TO FREEZE: the loaf freezes well and so I usually make three times the quantities given in this recipe, rounding the amount of lentils up to 500 g (1·1 lb) for convenience. I think it's best to freeze the loaf before cooking. Form the mixture into a loaf shape, coat with crumbs and open-freeze. Wrap when firm. To use, unwrap, thaw and then bake as above.

LENTIL SHEPHERD'S PIE

Continental lentils also make a tasty moist filling for a shepherd's pie. I find this a quick dish to make, if I can remember to save some mashed potato from a previous meal, and it only needs some savoury sauce (page 124) and a quickly cooked green vegetable such as baby sprouts or spinach to go with it. Leave out the wine, by the way, if you think it's extravagant, but if you can spare a little it does give a lovely flavour.

Serves 4–6
Calories: 395 if serving 4; 320 if serving 6

175 g (6 oz) brown lentils
550 ml (1 pint) water
1 bay leaf
1 onion, peeled and finely chopped
1 tablespoon oil
1 small carrot, peeled and chopped
1 stick of celery, finely chopped

1 garlic clove, crushed
4 tablespoons wine – any cheap kind will do
425 g (15 oz) can tomatoes
Sea salt and freshly ground black pepper
700 g (1½ lb) mashed potato
25 g (1 oz) grated cheese

Put the lentils, water and bay leaf into a medium-sized saucepan and leave to simmer gently until the lentils are tender – 45–60 minutes. Set the oven to 200°C (400°F), gas mark 6. Fry the onion in the oil for 10 minutes, then add the carrot, celery and garlic and cook for a further couple of minutes, stirring from time to time. Remove from the heat and stir in the wine and tomatoes; season to taste with salt and pepper. Spoon the mixture into a lightly greased shallow ovenproof dish and cover with the mashed potato. Level the surface, then rough it up with the prongs of a fork and sprinkle with the grated cheese. Bake for 45 minutes.

TO FREEZE: shepherd's pie freezes well and I find it worth making a double quantity and freezing half in an ovenproof container. To use, thaw then bake as above.

Cereals and Curries

LAZY GNOCCHI

This is a quick, lazy version of the Italian dish, gnocchi. You make a thick cheesy semolina mixture as usual but instead of spreading it out on a plate to cool then cutting it into shapes, you just pour the hot mixture into a shallow ovenproof dish, sprinkle the surface with cheese and grill or bake until crisp and golden. It looks and tastes almost the same and is delicious with just a well-dressed green salad or with tomato sauce and a lightly-cooked green vegetable.

You can get the wholewheat semolina at health shops.

Serves 4–6
Calories: 375 if serving 4; 250 if serving 6

575 ml (1 pint) liquid skimmed milk
1 bay leaf
1 onion stuck with a clove
175 g (6 oz) wholewheat semolina

150 g (6 oz) grated cheese
1 teaspoon mustard powder
Salt and freshly ground black pepper
1 tomato, sliced

Put the milk into a large saucepan with the bay leaf and the onion and bring to the boil. Remove from the heat, cover and leave for at least 10 minutes. Remove the bay leaf and onion. Bring milk up to the boil again then gradually sprinkle the semolina over the surface, stirring all the time, until you have a smooth, thick sauce. Let it cook over a gentle heat for 5 minutes, stirring often. Remove from the heat and stir in two-thirds of the cheese, the mustard and some salt and pepper. Pour the thick mixture into a shallow ovenproof dish so that it makes a layer not more than 1 cm ($\frac{1}{2}$ in) deep. Top with the rest of the cheese and the slices of tomato. Put under a hot grill for 10–15 minutes until bubbling underneath and golden brown and crisp on top. Serve at once.

If you want to take more trouble, a popular variation is to make this mixture into fritters. You won't need the extra cheese. Spread the mixture out about 5 mm ($\frac{1}{4}$ in) deep on a flat plate and leave to get completely cold. Cut into pieces. Dip each piece into beaten egg then into breadcrumbs – press to make the crumbs stick. Shallow fry quickly on both sides until lightly browned and crisp. Serve as soon as possible dusted with Parmesan. Serves 6 at about 350 calories a serving.

TO FREEZE: this mixture freezes well and if put into a suitable container can be cooked from frozen. The fritters also freeze excellently: open-freeze, store in a polythene bag when firm; fry from frozen.

NUTTY BROWN RICE WITH VEGETABLES

A dish of brown rice mixed with colourful vegetables and topped with shiny golden nuts always looks mouthwatering and inviting and isn't difficult to prepare. Leave out the ginger, chilli and coriander if you can't get them and use some basil or thyme instead. Serve the rice with a crisp salad and a sauce, too, if you like – tangy cheese sauce or sharp-tasting horseradish, lemon and mustard go well.

Serves 4
Calories: 440 in each serving

275 g (10 oz) long grain brown rice
500 ml (18 fl oz) water
Sea salt
1 medium-sized aubergine
2 large onions
3–4 garlic cloves

1 tablespoon oil
1 red pepper
350 g (12 oz) button mushrooms
$\frac{1}{2}$–1 green chilli if available
$\frac{1}{2}$–1 teaspoon grated fresh ginger, if available

1 teaspoon coriander seed, lightly crushed

2 tomatoes, peeled and roughly chopped

Freshly ground black pepper

125 g (4 oz) hazel nuts, roasted on a dry baking sheet in a moderate oven for about 20 minutes, until skins loosen and the nuts are golden

Put the rice into a medium-sized saucepan with the water and a teaspoonful of salt. Bring to the boil, then cover and cook very gently for 40–45 minutes, when the rice should be tender and all the water absorbed.

Wash the aubergine and remove the stalk. Cut the aubergine into fairly small dice, put them into a colander, sprinkle with salt and place a weight on top. Leave on one side while you prepare the rest of the vegetables.

Peel and chop the onions and peel and crush the garlic. Fry together in the oil in a large saucepan for 5 minutes, stirring quite often to prevent sticking. Remove stalk and seeds from the pepper and cut the flesh into dice; wash the mushrooms, cutting any larger ones. Cut the chilli in half and remove the seeds; finely chop the flesh. (Wash your hands thoroughly after preparing the chilli as the juice can sting if you get it on your face or in your eyes.) Drain the aubergine, rinse under the cold tap and squeeze it dry with your hands. Add the mushrooms, peppers, aubergine, chilli, ginger and coriander to the onions and fry for a further 5–10 minutes, until all the vegetables are soft. When the rice is cooked, stir it gently with a fork to 'fluff' it, then mix it lightly with the vegetables. Add the tomatoes and half the nuts and season well with salt and freshly ground black pepper. Serve with the rest of the nuts on top.

TO FREEZE: unsuitable.

CURRIED RICE AND CHEESE FRITTERS

If you have some cooked rice over, these fritters can be made very quickly. They are crisp on the outside, moist and tasty within. We like them with a crisp salad and natural yoghurt or one of the yoghurt/mayonnaise dressings in the sauces section, but they're also good with a tomato or curry sauce and a cooked vegetable. A pleasant variation is to add 2 chopped hardboiled eggs to the mixture.

Serves 4
Calories: 450 in each serving

About 450 g (1 lb) cooked brown rice – this is about 225 g (8 oz) uncooked
125 g (4 oz) grated cheese
2 teaspoons curry powder
2 eggs, beaten

Sea salt and freshly ground black pepper
50 g (2 oz) soft wholewheat breadcrumbs for coating
Oil for shallow frying

Mix together the cooked rice, grated cheese, curry powder and half the beaten egg. Season with salt and pepper. Form into croquettes, dip each in the rest of the beaten egg then coat with the breadcrumbs. Fry the croquettes quickly on both sides in the minimum of oil; drain well and serve as soon as possible.

TO FREEZE: open-freeze. Half thaw, then fry.

RISOTTO

A creamy risotto makes a delicious supper dish and is easy to prepare. If you can spare a little dry cider or wine for this it really does make all the difference to the flavour.

Serves 4
Calories: 485 in each serving

2 tablespoons sunflower oil
2 large onions, peeled and chopped
275 g (10 oz) long grain brown rice
300 ml ($\frac{1}{2}$ pint) dry cider or dry white wine

550 ml (1 pint) water
Sea salt
225 g (8 oz) button mushrooms
125 g (4 oz) grated cheese
Freshly ground black pepper

Heat half the oil in a large saucepan and fry the onions gently for 10 minutes, without browning. Add the rice, cider or wine, water and a teaspoonful of sea salt. Bring to the boil, cover, and leave to cook gently for 40 minutes. Towards the end of the cooking time, lightly fry the mushrooms in the remaining oil, then add them to the cooked rice, mixing lightly with a fork. Stir in the cheese and check the seasoning. Serve with a crisp green salad with a good olive oil and wine vinegar dressing, or with a tomato and onion salad, and some chilled white wine or cider.

TO FREEZE: unsuitable.

SPICY LENTIL DAHL WITH SAMBALS

This is a surprisingly quick dish to make and always seems popular with its accompanying 'sambals' or little bowls of colourful ingredients. If you're planning to serve it with rice, it's a good idea to get this on to cook before starting on the dahl, so that they're ready at the same time.

Serves 4
Calories: 220 in each serving; rice and sambals extra

225 g (8 oz) split red lentils
1 bay leaf
550 ml (1 pint) water
1 large onion, peeled and chopped
1 small cooking apple, peeled and chopped
1 garlic clove, peeled and crushed

1 tablespoon oil
½–1 teaspoon sea salt
¼ teaspoon pepper
1–2 teaspoons curry paste or powder
1 tablespoon lemon juice

For the sambals:
Some or all of the following, in little bowls – diced cucumber, grated carrot, chopped cabbage and raisins, sliced banana, sliced tomato and onion, flaked almonds, desiccated coconut, mango chutney

Put the lentils, bay leaf and water into a medium-sized saucepan

101

and simmer gently until tender – about 20 minutes. Remove bay leaf. Meanwhile fry the onion, apple and garlic in the oil for 10 minutes. Add the onion mixture to the lentils, together with the remaining ingredients. You can liquidize the mixture at this point if you want to, or leave it as it is. I prefer it liquidized. Reheat the dahl gently and serve with fluffy brown rice and sambals.

TO FREEZE: the lentil dahl freezes well. To use, allow plenty of time for the mixture to thaw, then heat very gently. It is easiest to heat it through in a covered dish in a low oven to prevent problems with the mixture sticking and burning in a saucepan.

VEGETABLE BIRIANI

This is a lovely curry dish: spicy golden rice garnished with slices of tomato and hardboiled egg and served with a tasty curry sauce. I have a passion for the strange, glutinous texture of okra, or ladies' fingers (which Indians call *bhindi*). This is quite often available fresh these days, but if you can't get it you could use a can, or substitute the same quantity of French beans or courgettes and add with the peas.

Serves 4
Calories: in each serving 340

1 onion, peeled and chopped
1 large garlic clove, peeled and crushed
1 tablespoon oil
1 bay leaf
2 teaspoons turmeric
4–5 cardamom pods
Piece of cinnamon stick
Pinch of ground cloves
1–2 teaspoons sea salt
275 g (10 oz) long grain brown rice

125 g (4 oz) okra, washed and trimmed if necessary
500 ml (18 fl oz) water
125 g (4 oz) frozen peas
1 tomato, sliced
1 hardboiled egg, sliced
½ punnet mustard and cress, washed

Fry the onion and garlic in the oil for 10 minutes, then stir in the bay leaf, spices and salt. Add the rice, okra, turmeric and water and bring up to the boil. Put a lid on the saucepan, turn the heat right down and leave to cook very gently for 40 minutes. Alternatively the biriani can be cooked in the oven for 40 minutes at 200°C (400°F), gas mark 6. 10 minutes before the rice is ready, add the peas – just tip them on top without stirring. When the rice is ready remove the saucepan from the heat and leave it to stand, still covered, for 10 minutes. Then fork the rice through lightly and serve it piled up on a warmed serving dish garnished with the slices of tomato and egg, and the cress. Serve it with mango chutney, poppadums and the following sauce.

TO FREEZE: biriani freezes well, without the tomato, egg and cress. Store in a polythene bag. When you want to use the biriani it's best to let it thaw completely then heat it through in a covered casserole dish in a low oven.

VEGETABLE CURRY SAUCE
FOR BIRIANI

Don't be put off by the long list of spices in this recipe; the method is very quick and easy.

Serves 4
Calories: about 170 in each serving

2 medium-sized onions, peeled and chopped
4 garlic cloves, peeled and crushed
1 tablespoon oil
2 teaspoons curry paste or powder
1 teaspoon paprika pepper
½ teaspoon turmeric
1 teaspoon garam masala

225 g (8 oz) can tomatoes
1 tablespoon tomato paste
300 ml (½ pint) water
Sea salt, freshly ground black pepper, a drop of honey
125 g (4 oz) okra, washed and trimmed as necessary
450 g (1 lb) potatoes, peeled and cut into even-sized chunks

Fry the onion and garlic in the oil for 10 minutes, then add all the spices. Cook for 1 minute, then stir in the tomatoes, tomato paste, water and a little salt and pepper. Taste and add a very little honey if necessary. Bring up to the boil, then put in the vegetables and simmer gently for about 25 minutes, until the potatoes are cooked. Check seasoning. Serve with the biriani.

TO FREEZE: you can freeze the sauce without the potatoes and okra. To use, thaw, put into a saucepan with some prepared potatoes and okra and simmer gently for about 25 minutes, as above.

Flans, Pizzas and Pies

Can flans and pastries ever be considered healthy, in view of the amount of fat they contain? They can if you adapt traditional recipes and methods a little and provided you plan the rest of the meal carefully.

Use 100 per cent wholewheat flour and polyunsaturated margarine for the pastry. It's easiest to mix this with a fork and roll it out on a lightly floured board; slide the pastry straight from the board to the tin or dish. You won't get so many crumbles this way, but if the pastry does break, just push it together again – no one will mind a few patches if it tastes good! And for flan fillings, try replacing cream with smooth white fromage blanc. This gives a deliciously rich-tasting result, similar to cream but much healthier.

Even if you're serving a healthy flan or pie, it's a good idea to keep the fat in the rest of the meal – and in the day's eating generally – to the minimum.

So start the meal with a salad or vegetable dish such as marinated mushrooms, creamy butter bean dip or stuffed tomatoes. Or try one of the low-fat soups: easy tomato or chilled cucumber, for instance. Serve the flan or pie with a lightly-dressed salad or plainly cooked vegetables, and finish with a refreshing fruity pudding such as pineapple and orange compote.

BUTTER BEAN AND CHUTNEY ROLL

Melt-in-the-mouth wholewheat pastry, onions, butter beans and sweet chutney make a tasty savoury roll. Serve it hot, and keep the rest of the meal – and the day's eating generally – low in fat.

Serves 4

Calories: 470 in each serving with mango chutney, about 430 with sugarless chutney

150 g (6 oz) wholewheat flour
1 slightly rounded teaspoon baking powder
Sea salt
75 g (3 oz) polyunsaturated margarine
1 tablespoon water
2 large onions, peeled and thinly sliced
1 tablespoon oil
100 g (3–4 oz) butter beans, soaked, rinsed and cooked, or use a 425 g (15 oz) can
2 rounded tablespoons sweet chutney – mango chutney or the sugarless one in the preserves section
1 teaspoon dried basil
Freshly ground pepper
Milk or beaten egg for glazing if liked

First make the pastry. Sift the flour, baking powder and a pinch of salt into a bowl; add also the residue of bran from the sieve. Mix in the soft margarine using a fork. When the mixture looks like fairly coarse breadcrumbs add the water and mix to a dough. Leave pastry to rest while you make the filling.

Set the oven to 200°C (400°F), gas mark 6. Fry the onion in the oil for about 10 minutes, until it's soft, stirring quite often to prevent it sticking. Drain the butter beans and mix them with the onion, together with the chutney, basil and a seasoning of salt and pepper.

Roll the pastry into an oval about 30 × 25 cm (12 × 10 in) and spoon the butter bean mixture on to the centre. Brush the edges of the pastry with a little cold water and bring the sides of the pastry up to the centre, pressing them together and making an attractive join, so that it looks like a large Cornish pasty. Brush with a little milk or beaten egg if you like, then bake the roll for 30–35 minutes, until golden brown. I would serve this with a green vegetable, mashed potatoes and the savoury sauce from the sauces section.

TO FREEZE: open-freeze the roll before cooking, then pack carefully in a rigid container. To use, remove from container and place on a baking sheet. Leave until defrosted, then bake as above.

CHEESE AND ONION FLAN

This is a good flan, a tasty mixture of cheese, mustard and onion on a crisp wholewheat pastry base. It's quite quick to make and popular with all the family.

Serves 6
Calories: 280 in each serving

150 g (6 oz) wholewheat flour
75 g (3 oz) polyunsaturated
  margarine
1 tablespoon water
2 large onions, peeled and
  finely chopped
125 g (4 oz) fromage blanc
1 teaspoon Dijon mustard

2 eggs
1–2 tablespoons chopped
  parsley
Sea salt and freshly ground
  black pepper
25 g (1 oz) grated cheese
Dried basil
1 tomato, sliced

Preheat the oven to 200°C (400°F), gas mark 6. Sift the flour into a bowl, adding also the residue of bran from the sieve. Using a fork, work in the margarine until the mixture looks like rather coarse breadcrumbs, then add the water and mix to a dough. Roll out the dough on a lightly floured board and use to line a 20 cm (8 in) flan dish. Prick the base and bake in the oven for 15 minutes, until well set and lightly browned. Turn the heat down to 190°C (375°F), gas mark 5.

While the flan case is cooking, make the filling. Put the onions, fromage blanc, mustard, eggs and parsley into a bowl and mix well together. Season with salt and pepper. Spoon the mixture into the cooked flan case – it doesn't matter if the flan case is still hot. Sprinkle with the grated cheese and a little basil and arrange the slices of tomato attractively on top. Bake for 30 minutes.

This is good served hot with a cooked vegetable such as French beans and frozen peas and some tomato sauce, or with one of the mixtures from the salads and vegetables section – the carrot, apple, celery and raisin one goes well with it.

TO FREEZE: cook the flan as described, cool, then open-freeze, pack and store. To use, defrost completely, then gently heat through.

MUSHROOM FLAN

This is a rich, luxurious-tasting flan yet it's considerably lower in fat and calories than a traditional creamy flan. Serve it when you have planned low-fat meals for the rest of the day's eating.

Serves 6
Calories: 260 in each serving

150 g (6 oz) wholewheat flour
75 g (3 oz) polyunsaturated
  margarine
1 tablespoon water
1 small onion, peeled and
  finely chopped
1 teaspoon oil
Small garlic clove, peeled and
  crushed

175 g (6 oz) button
  mushrooms, washed and
  sliced
125 g (4 oz) fromage blanc
1 egg
1 tablespoon chopped parsley
Sea salt and freshly ground
  black pepper

Prepare the pastry and make a flan case as described above, baking at 200° C (400°F), gas mark 6, for 10–15 minutes, until golden and crisp. While the flan case is cooking, make the filling. Fry the onion in the oil for 4–5 minutes, stirring frequently, then add the garlic and mushrooms and fry for a further 2 minutes. Remove from heat and stir in the fromage blanc, egg, parsley and salt and pepper to taste. Spoon the mixture into the flan case and bake for 30 minutes, until set. Serve hot or cold, with a salad or light mashed potatoes and a plainly cooked vegetable.

TO FREEZE: this flan freezes well. Bake as described, cool and open-freeze. Pack carefully. To use, remove wrappings, put the flan on a baking sheet or ovenproof plate and leave to thaw. Warm through before serving.

SPINACH TART

Chopped green spinach and creamy fromage blanc make a lovely, low-fat filling for a flan and go particularly well with the nutty flavour of wholewheat pastry. It's best served hot and is good with a salad, such as the tomato and onion one or with cooked vegetables, in which case I think the tomato sauce or the horseradish, lemon and mustard sauce go well with it and make an attractive colour contrast.

Serves 4–6
Calories: 380 a portion if serving 4; 255 if serving 6

150 g (6 oz) wholewheat flour
75 g (3 oz) polyunsaturated
  margarine
1 tablespoon water
300 g (11 oz) packet frozen
  chopped spinach, or 450 g
  (1 lb) fresh spinach, washed,
  cooked and finely chopped

75 g (3 oz) fromage blanc
Grated nutmeg
Sea salt and freshly ground
  black pepper
25 g (1 oz) finely grated cheese
1 small tomato

Set oven to 200°C (400°F), gas mark 6. Make the pastry: sift the flour into a fairly large bowl, adding also the residue of bran left in the sieve. Add the fat and mix with a fork until the mixture resembles breadcrumbs, then add the water and gather mixture into a dough. Roll out thinly and line an 18–20 cm (7–8 in) flan dish or tin; prick base. Bake the flan in the oven for about 15 minutes, until golden and very crisp.

While the flan case is cooking, make the filling. Mix together the spinach, fromage blanc, a good grating of nutmeg, and some salt and freshly ground pepper. Spoon the spinach mixture into the flan and smooth the surface; finish with the grated cheese and decorate with the slices of tomato. Return the flan to the oven, reduce heat to 190°C (375°F), gas mark 5, and bake for a further 30 minutes.

TO FREEZE: spinach tart freezes well: follow directions given for freezing the mushroom flan above.

QUICK BREAD PIZZA

An oval wholewheat loaf, split in half, makes a lovely crisp, crunchy base for a quick pizza. I like to top the bread with lots of fried onion, tomato, cheese and black olives. If you have a freezer and keep a couple of these loaves in it, already split as described in the recipe, you can make this pizza in next to no time.

Serves 4
Calories: 340 in each serving

1 oval wholewheat loaf, about 450 g (1 lb)
2 large onions, peeled and sliced
1 tablespoon oil
2 very large tomatoes, weighing about 450 g (1 lb) together, or a 425 g (15 oz) can

Sea salt and freshly ground black pepper
Dried basil or oregano
125 g (4 oz) grated Cheshire cheese
8 black olives

Set the oven to 200°C (400°F), gas mark 6. Slice the loaf in half lengthwise and scoop out the soft crumb – this won't be needed, but can be made into breadcrumbs and used in other recipes. Fry the onions in the oil for 10 minutes, until soft and lightly browned. Put the two halves of the loaf on a baking sheet and cover with the onions. Slice the tomatoes, if you're using fresh ones, or drain canned tomatoes. Arrange the tomatoes on top of the onions and season well with salt and pepper. Sprinkle with the cheese and herbs and bake for 20 minutes, until the crust is very crisp and the cheese melted and beginning to brown. Decorate with the olives and serve immediately, with a crisp green salad or an easily cooked vegetable such as frozen green beans or peas.

TO FREEZE: if you use canned tomatoes for this you can freeze it after assembling but before cooking. But it doesn't take very long to make the topping and I think the best plan is to keep a couple of the wholewheat loaves in the freezer, with the crumb already scooped out. These can then be used straight from the freezer, without defrosting, when you're in a hurry.

Pasta and Pancakes

Some of the most warming, satisfying dishes come into this section and the macaroni and spaghetti ones are all quick and easy to make.

Wholewheat pasta can be bought from health shops and many supermarkets. Like brown rice, although it looks quite dauntingly dark in the pack, it's much lighter when it's cooked.

To cook wholewheat pasta perfectly, half fill a large saucepan with water and add a teaspoonful of salt. Bring to the boil then put in the pasta, gently easing the long varieties, spaghetti and lasagne, into the water as they soften. Let the pasta bubble away without a lid on the saucepan until it's tender but not soggy – bite a piece to see. The time on the packet will be a guide, but I find the pasta doesn't always take as long as it says.

Tip the pasta into a colander to drain, then (except for lasagne) put it back into the saucepan: there's no need to rinse the pasta in either hot or cold water. Add a little oil or margarine, some salt and freshly ground black pepper. With lasagne, after draining drape the pieces over the sides of the colander to keep them separate until you need them.

LENTIL LASAGNE

This dish consists of layers of lasagne with a tasty mixture of onion, mushroom and lentil, and cottage and cheddar cheese. It's not much bother to make and only needs a salad to accompany it.

Serves 4–6
Calories: 515 a portion if serving 4; 350 if serving 6

175 g (6 oz) wholewheat lasagne
1 onion, peeled and chopped
1 tablespoon oil
125 g (4 oz) mushrooms, wiped and chopped
425 g (15 oz) can tomatoes
125 g (4 oz) split red lentils
150 ml ($\frac{1}{4}$ pint) stock or red wine
3 large garlic cloves, peeled and crushed
$\frac{1}{2}$ teaspoon each dried basil, thyme, oregano and marjoram
Sea salt and freshly ground black pepper
225 g (8 oz) cottage cheese
125 g (4 oz) grated Cheddar cheese
A few breadcrumbs, a little Parmesan cheese

Cook the lasagne in a large saucepan half filled with boiling salted water; drain and drape the lasagne over the sides of the colander so they don't stick together while you prepare the filling. Fry the onion in the oil for 7 minutes, add the mushrooms and cook for a further 3 minutes, then stir in the tomatoes, lentils, water or wine and crushed garlic. Cook gently for 20-30 minutes, until the lentils are very tender. Add the herbs and season to taste. Set oven to 200°C (400°F), gas mark 6.

Put a layer of the lentil mixture in the base of a lightly-greased shallow casserole dish, cover this with some pieces of lasagne followed by another layer of lentils, some cottage cheese, some grated cheese then lasagne; continue in layers like this until everything is used. Sprinkle the top with some crumbs and grated Parmesan cheese and bake in the oven for 1 hour.

TO FREEZE: this dish freezes well. Prepare as above but do not bake. To use, allow plenty of time for thawing, preferably overnight, then bake as described above.

MACARONI AND MUSHROOM BAKE

This is a useful dish because it's quick to make, and freezes well. It really only needs a salad or frozen peas to accompany it though my family prefer it with a quick tomato sauce as well.

Serves 4
Calories: 315 in each serving

125 g (4 oz) wholewheat
   macaroni
Sea salt
2 medium-sized onions, peeled
   and chopped
1 tablespoon oil
125 g (4 oz) mushrooms,
   washed and chopped

225 g (8 oz) tomatoes,
   skinned and chopped
1 egg, beaten
125 g (4 oz) grated cheese
Freshly ground black pepper
25 g (1 oz) fresh wholewheat
   crumbs

Half fill a fairly large saucepan with water, add a teaspoonful
of salt and bring to the boil. Tip in the macaroni and boil, uncovered, for about 10 minutes, until the macaroni feels tender
but still has a little 'bite' to it. Drain. Set the oven to 190°C
(375°F), gas mark 5.

While the macaroni is cooking, fry the onions in the oil for
7 minutes, then add the mushrooms and tomatoes and cook for
a further 3 minutes. Pour in the beaten egg and cook for a minute
or two longer, stirring, until the egg has set. Remove from the
heat and add the macaroni and grated cheese. Taste and season
with salt and freshly ground black pepper. Spoon the mixture into
a shallow ovenproof dish and sprinkle with the crumbs. Bake for
25–30 minutes, until hot, bubbling and crisped on top.

TO FREEZE: freeze before baking. Thaw, then cook as above.
Macaroni and mushroom bake freezes well and I find it worthwhile to make a double batch.

RED BEAN LASAGNE

A moist mixture of red kidney beans and tomatoes makes a
delicious filling for lasagne.

Serves 6
Calories: 390 per serving

150 g (6 oz) wholewheat
  lasagne
Sea salt
1 large onion, peeled and
  chopped
1 tablespoon oil
150 g (6 oz) red kidney
  beans, soaked, cooked for
  $1-1\frac{1}{4}$ hours until tender, or

use 2 tins of red kidney
  beans
225 g (8 oz) can tomatoes
2 tablespoons tomato paste
1 teaspoon powdered
  cinnamon
Freshly ground black pepper
  and a dash of honey

*For the cheese sauce and
  topping:*
25 g (1 oz) polyunsaturated
  margarine
50 g (2 oz) flour

575 ml (1 pint) skimmed milk
125 g (4 oz) strongly-flavoured
  cheese, grated

Half fill a large saucepan with water and add a teaspoonful of salt.
Bring to the boil, then put in the lasagne, easing it in gently as
it softens in the water. Boil the lasagne, without a lid on the
saucepan, for about 10 minutes, until tender. Drain the lasagne
and drape the pieces over the sides of the saucepan to prevent
them sticking together while you prepare the filling.

Fry the onion in the oil in a medium-sized saucepan for 10
minutes, until tender. Drain the beans, keeping the liquid. Add
the beans to the onions, mashing them a little to break them up,
also the tomatoes, tomato paste, cinnamon, salt, freshly ground
black pepper and a very little honey to taste if you think the
mixture needs it.

Make a low-fat cheese sauce. The easiest way to do this is to
put the margarine, flour and milk into the liquidizer goblet and
blend for a minute, then transfer the mixture to a saucepan and
stir over a moderate heat until thickened. Otherwise, melt the
margarine in the saucepan and stir in the flour as usual, then
add the milk and stir over the heat until thickened. Stir in half
the cheese and season to taste.

Set the oven to 200° C (400°F), gas mark 6. Put a layer of the
bean mixture into a shallow ovenproof dish and cover with some
pieces of lasagne; follow this with another layer of the bean
mixture, then more lasagne and any remaining beans. Then pour
the cheese sauce over the top and sprinkle with the rest of the
cheese. Bake for about 45 minutes, until golden and bubbling.

Serve with a simply cooked green vegetable, or, better I think, a crisp green salad, such as the watercress, celery and lettuce one.

TO FREEZE: you can freeze this. See instructions given for the lentil lasagne.

SPAGHETTI WITH LENTILS AND RED PEPPER

I love this combination of flavours and textures and this recipe has the advantage of being very easy to make. You could use either continental lentils or, my preference, split red lentils, for the sauce. And if you don't like red peppers, you could replace them with more tomato or mushrooms.

Serves 4
Calories: 400 a serving, without the Parmesan

1 large onion, peeled and
   chopped
2 tablespoons olive oil
2 garlic cloves, peeled and
   crushed
1 large red pepper, washed,
   de-seeded and chopped
125 g (4 oz) split red lentils
225 g (8 oz) tomatoes,
   skinned, or use a small can

250 ml (8 fl oz) water
1 tablespoon tomato paste
½ teaspoon paprika pepper
Sea salt and freshly ground
   black pepper
225 g (8 oz) wholewheat
   spaghetti

To serve: A little grated Parmesan cheese

Fry the onion in a medium-sized saucepan in half the oil until tender – 10 minutes. Add half the garlic, the red pepper, lentils and tomatoes and cook for a further 1–2 minutes, then add the water. Bring to the boil and simmer gently for 20 minutes, until the lentils are tender. Add the tomato paste and paprika and season well with salt and freshly ground black pepper.

Half fill a large saucepan with water, add a teaspoonful of salt and bring to the boil. Put the spaghetti into the saucepan, easing it down into the water gradually as it softens. Boil the spaghetti for about 10 minutes, until when you taste a piece it is tender but still has some 'bite' to it. Drain the spaghetti then put it back into the saucepan with the rest of the oil and garlic and a good grinding of black pepper. Turn the spaghetti lightly in the saucepan so that it all gets coated with the oil and garlic, then serve it with the lentil sauce, some Parmesan cheese and a crisp green salad.

TO FREEZE: You can freeze the lentil mixture. Cool, put into a rigid container, freeze and label. To use, thaw, then heat gently, stirring frequently.

PANCAKES STUFFED WITH SPINACH AND BASIL

I like spinach in almost any form and I think it makes a particularly good filling for pancakes, being light, moist and tasty. I must admit I quite often use frozen spinach for this recipe, which makes it very quick, but you could of course use fresh spinach instead if you prefer.

Serves 6
Calories: 320 in each portion

For the filling:
2 300 g (11 oz) packets frozen spinach, thawed, or 900 g (2 lb) fresh spinach
2 teaspoons tomato paste
1–2 teaspoons dried basil
Sea salt and freshly ground black pepper

For the pancakes:
125 g (4 oz) plain wholewheat flour
A pinch of salt
2 eggs
1 tablespoon vegetable oil
200 ml (7 fl oz) skimmed milk

To finish:
700 ml (1¼ pints) tangy cheese sauce, p. 121
50 g (2 oz) grated cheese

If you're using frozen spinach, put it into a colander and leave to drain; if you're using fresh spinach, wash it thoroughly, then cook

116

it in a large saucepan with just the water clinging to it, until tender – about 10 minutes. Drain and chop. Add the tomato paste and basil to the spinach and season well.

Next make the pancakes. The easiest way to do this is to put all the ingredients into the liquidizer and simply blend until smooth. Otherwise, put the flour and salt into a bowl, break in the eggs and beat, then gradually mix in the oil and milk until you've got a smooth, creamy consistency.

Set a small frying pan over a moderate heat and brush it lightly with oil. When it is hot pour in enough pancake batter to coat the base of the frying pan thinly. Tip and swirl the frying pan so that the batter runs all over the base. Then put the frying pan over the heat for 20–30 seconds until the top of the pancake is set and the base flecked with brown. Flip the pancake over using a small palette knife and your fingers if necessary. Cook the other side of the pancake, then lift it out on to a plate.

Brush the frying pan with more oil if necessary (I find with a non-stick frying pan I only have to do this after about every three pancakes) and make another pancake in the same way, putting it on top of the first when it's done. Continue until all the mixture is used up and you have a pile of about 12 or 15 pancakes. (You can do this in advance if you wish.)

Set the oven to 200°C (400°F), mark 6. Put a good spoonful of spinach on each pancake and roll the pancake up; place the pancakes side by side in a shallow ovenproof dish. When they're all in, pour the cheese sauce evenly over the top and sprinkle with the remaining cheese. Bake for 45 minutes. These are good served with creamy mashed potatoes and grilled or baked tomatoes.

TO FREEZE: you can freeze this dish already assembled, or freeze the pancakes and sauce separately. Whichever you do, thaw completely before assembling/baking.

PANCAKES STUFFED WITH TOMATOES AND HAZEL NUTS

This may sound rather unusual, but we like this combination of flavours and textures very much and I find it's popular with most people.

Serves 6

Calories: about 400 in each serving

12–15 thin wholewheat
pancakes, made as in the
previous recipe

For the filling:

6 tomatoes, skinned and
chopped, or a 425 g (15 oz)
can

175 g (6 oz) fresh wholewheat
bread, crusts removed

1 large onion, peeled and
finely chopped

1 tablespoon vegetable oil

1 garlic clove, peeled and
crushed

125 g (4 oz) hazel nuts,
roasted in a moderate oven
for 20 minutes, then
pulverized in the liquidizer

1 teaspoon dried thyme

1 tablespoon tomato paste

2–3 tablespoons red wine,
optional

Sea salt, freshly ground black
pepper, a dash of honey

To finish:

700 ml (1¼ pints) tangy cheese
sauce, p. 121

50 g (2 oz) grated cheese

Make the pancakes as in the previous recipe and leave on one side. To make the filling, chop the tomatoes and put into a bowl with the bread; mash the bread into the tomatoes with a fork and leave for 10 minutes to allow the bread to soften, mashing it with a fork once or twice more. Set the oven to 200°C (400°F), gas mark 6.

Fry the onion in the oil for 10 minutes, then add this to the tomato and bread mixture, together with the garlic, nuts, thyme, tomato paste, wine if you're using it, and salt and pepper to taste, and maybe just a very little honey to bring out the flavour of the tomatoes.

Divide this mixture between the pancakes, rolling them up and putting them side by side in a shallow ovenproof dish. Pour the cheese sauce over the top, sprinkle with the grated cheese and bake for 45 minutes. These pancakes are good with a cooked green vegetable, such as spinach, and mashed potatoes or a green salad.

TO FREEZE: you can freeze the complete dish, uncooked, or prepare the pancakes, filling and sauce and freeze them separately. Thaw, then assemble and/or cook as described above.

Sauces and Salad Dressings

Sauces and salad dressings can add a great deal of fat to a meal if you're not careful, yet it's surprising how much you can reduce this, without spoiling the flavour, once you think about it.

For instance, although I think olive oil is indispensable with many salads, if you use a really good quality one you don't need nearly as much.

Although mayonnaise is horribly high in calories – around 200 for a slightly rounded tablespoonful (28 g [1 oz]) – you can halve the calories by mixing it with natural yoghurt. Or, better still, we've found you can make beautiful creamy dressings, which taste very much like mayonnaise, using white cheese and yoghurt. These dressings contain only a fraction of the calories of mayonnaise yet don't seem any less rich to eat.

Fresh fruit juices are useful for moistening some salads, such as grated carrot, and I also like bought fat-free French dressing on a shredded cabbage salad.

You can make some delicious low-fat sauces by simply puréeing cooked vegetables. And you can reduce the calories in flour-thickened sauces if you leave out the fat and use skimmed milk instead of whole milk.

MAYONNAISE AND YOGHURT

You can use either home-made mayonnaise or a good quality bought one for this.

Serves 4
Calories: 107 in each serving

2 tablespoons mayonnaise   2 tablespoons natural yoghurt

Simply mix everything together.

TO FREEZE: unsuitable.

119

WHITE MAYONNAISE

My daughter Margaret invented this dressing and it's a great favourite with us all. We think it tastes very much like mayonnaise but only contains a fraction of the calories. You can vary the flavour by adding ½ teaspoonful of Dijon mustard and you can also add a little liquid skimmed milk if you want a thinner consistency.

Serves 6–8
Calories: 35 in each portion if serving 8, 45 if serving 6

2 tablespoons natural yoghurt	½ teaspoon wine vinegar
125 g (4 oz) curd cheese	Sea salt and freshly ground
2 teaspoons olive oil	black pepper

Simply mix everything together to a smooth cream.

TO FREEZE: unsuitable.

CURRIED YOGHURT MAYONNAISE

My idea with this recipe was to try and make something which was a little like a rich curried mayonnaise, but without the calories. It's especially good with hardboiled eggs, bean salads and with rice or lentil fritters

Makes about 375 ml (½ pint), serves 6–8
Calories: 80 a portion if serving 6; 60 if serving 8

1 tablespoon oil	6 tablespoons red wine
1 small onion, peeled and finely chopped	150 g (5 oz) natural yoghurt
2 teaspoons curry powder	150 g (5 oz) fromage blanc
1 teaspoon tomato paste	Sea salt and freshly ground
1 teaspoon honey	black pepper

Heat the oil in a small saucepan and gently fry the onion until tender – 10 minutes. Stir in the curry powder, tomato paste, honey and wine and bubble over a high heat until the liquid has reduced to a thick syrup. Remove from heat and leave to get completely cold, sieve and add the yoghurt and fromage blanc, or liquidize them all together to a creamy consistency. Season with salt and pepper.

TO FREEZE: unsuitable.

YOGHURT AND GREEN HERB DRESSING

This is a fresh-tasting, slightly sharp dressing that's good with most salad mixtures.

Serves 6
Calories: 15 in each serving

150 ml (5 fl oz) natural yoghurt
1 tablespoon lemon juice
Sea salt, freshly ground black pepper, maybe a dash of honey

1–2 tablespoons chopped green herbs or spring onions

Put the yoghurt into a bowl, add all the remaining ingredients and mix everything together. Season lightly with salt and pepper and a very little honey, just to take off some of the sharpness if necessary.

TO FREEZE: unsuitable.

TANGY CHEESE SAUCE

Use 400 ml ($\frac{3}{4}$ pint) milk for a pouring sauce; 275 ml ($\frac{1}{2}$ pint) for a thicker, coating sauce.

Serves 4
Calories: 110–190 depending on amount of cheese used

2 tablespoons unbleached
  white flour
275–400 ml ($\frac{1}{2}$–$\frac{3}{4}$ pint)
  skimmed milk
$\frac{1}{2}$ teaspoon dried thyme
2 teaspoons Dijon mustard

1 bay leaf
50–125 g (2–4 oz) grated
  cheese
Salt and freshly ground black
  pepper

Put the flour, milk, thyme and mustard into the liquidizer goblet and blend for 1 minute, then transfer to a medium-sized saucepan and add the bay leaf. Stir over the heat for a minute or two, until thickened, then leave to simmer very gently for about 7 minutes, to cook the flour. Add the cheese and season to taste.

TO FREEZE: Cool, pour into a rigid container, label and freeze. To use, thaw completely, heat very gently, stirring all the time.

HORSERADISH, LEMON AND MUSTARD SAUCE

This pleasantly sharp-tasting sauce is made in exactly the same way as a pouring cheese sauce above except that you leave out the cheese and add $\frac{1}{2}$–1 teaspoon horseradish sauce and the juice of half a lemon.

Serves 4
Calories: 75 in each serving

TO FREEZE: as above

MUSHROOM SAUCE

Make as for a pouring cheese sauce but use 75–125 g (3–4 oz) white button mushrooms instead of the cheese. Put the mushrooms into the liquidizer with the flour and milk, then continue as above. You can flavour this with the mustard or use a little grated nutmeg or powdered mace instead, and plenty of freshly ground black pepper.

Calories: 75 in each serving.

TO FREEZE: as above

PARSLEY SAUCE

You can also make a good parsley sauce using the method above. Take the stalks off several sprigs of parsley. Put the sprigs into the liquidizer with the flour, 400 ml (¾ pint) milk and blend. It's best with a generous amount of parsley so that it's beautifully green and fresh-tasting. Leave out the cheese and mustard but season well.

Calories: 75 in each serving.

TO FREEZE: as above.

RICH MUSHROOM SAUCE

Don't be alarmed by the quantity of garlic in this sauce: you hardly taste it at all. For a creamier sauce you can stir in a couple of tablespoonfuls of fromage blanc before serving, but don't let the sauce boil after this or it will spoil.

Serves 4
Calories: about 65 in each serving when made with wine

6 large garlic cloves, peeled but not crushed
1 tablespoon oil
225 g (8 oz) mushrooms, washed and sliced

75–150 ml (2½–5 fl oz) wine or stock
Sea salt and freshly ground black pepper

Put the garlic into a saucepan with the oil and the mushrooms and cook gently for 5 minutes, then tip everything into the liquidizer and blend until smooth. Put the mushroom mixture back into the saucepan and stir in the yoghurt or fromage blanc and enough wine or stock to make a fairly thick but pourable consistency. Season with salt and pepper.

TO FREEZE: unsuitable.

SAVOURY SAUCE

This is a useful everyday sauce but it can be made a bit special by replacing half the water with some wine.

Serves 4
Calories 50 in each serving

1 tablespoon oil
1 tablespoon wholewheat
  flour
2 teaspoons tomato paste

300 ml (½ pint) water
1 vegetable stock cube
1 bay leaf
Freshly ground black pepper

Heat the oil in a medium-sized saucepan and stir in the flour; cook for a minute or two over a moderate heat, then add the tomato paste. Add the water, stock cube and bay leaf and stir until thickened. Turn the heat down and leave to simmer gently for 5 minutes. Season with some freshly ground black pepper.

TO FREEZE: pour into a rigid container, cool, freeze, label. To use, thaw, then heat gently, stirring frequently.

TOMATO SAUCE

This is one of my standbys, being easy to make, low in fat and generally popular. If you prefer you could use fresh tomatoes instead of canned.

Serves 4–6
Calories: 50–60 a serving

1 medium-sized onion, peeled
  and chopped
1 tablespoon oil
425 g (15 oz) can tomatoes

1–2 teaspoons tomato paste
Sea salt, freshly ground black
  pepper, a little honey
½ teaspoon paprika – optional

Fry the onion in the oil in a medium-sized saucepan for 10
minutes, but don't let it get brown. Add the tomatoes and liquidize
the mixture. Add the tomato paste, some salt and pepper to taste
and just a little honey if necessary. The paprika is a pleasant
addition; so too is a little red wine, just 2 or 3 tablespoons, when
available.

TO FREEZE: this sauce freezes well. Cool, pour into a rigid
container, label and freeze. To use, defrost, then heat very gently,
stirring often.

Side Salads and Vegetables

The most important thing with almost all vegetables, and particularly with cauliflower and leafy green vegetables, is to cook them in the minimum amount of water for as short a time as possible. For green vegetables to serve 4 people you don't need more than 1 cm ($\frac{1}{2}$ in) water and it should be boiling when you put the vegetables in. It also helps if you cut the vegetables up well before cooking: sprouts are much better if they're halved or quartered as they don't get at all soggy this way, and cauliflower is best broken into small sprigs.

The vegetables should be only just tender – I think the Italian term for pasta *al dente*, on the tooth, is a good one to apply to vegetables, too. And remember that vegetables go on cooking in their own heat even after they've been drained.

If vegetables are properly cooked like this, they don't need lots of butter on them in order to taste good. A little sea salt, a grinding of black pepper and maybe a squeeze of lemon juice or a little chopped fresh parsley are fine for every day, with perhaps a little unsalted polyunsaturated margarine for special occasions.

These days I find I'm serving a side salad with our meals more and more. They're quick and easy to make and refreshing to eat, often providing just the right texture to set the meal off perfectly. Practically all the salads in this section are easy and require the minimum of effort to make – I don't think any of them are more trouble to do than cooking a vegetable and there's no saucepan to wash up afterwards, either.

As most of the recipes in this section are unsuitable for freezing, I've only given instructions for freezing where they apply.

CABBAGE, CELERY AND APPLE SALAD

Crisp white cabbage is so useful for salads in the winter, but it does need cheering along with other interesting ingredients. This is a good combination: cabbage with crisp celery and sweet apples, preferably Russets, when they're in season.

Serves 4
Calories: 65 with yoghurt; 45 with low-fat dressing, 50 with orange juice, per serving.

350 g (12 oz) white cabbage
1 head of celery
2 dessert apples

6 tablespoons low-fat French dressing, orange juice or natural yoghurt

Chop up the cabbage and put it into a large bowl. Slice the celery; chop the apples, discarding the core. Add the celery and apples to the cabbage together with the dressing of your choice. Mix well and serve as soon as possible.

CABBAGE AND PINEAPPLE SALAD

Most supermarkets now sell pineapple which has been canned in its own juice and it's lovely mixed with chopped white cabbage. The pineapple adds sweetness and the juice provides the dressing.

Serves 4
Calories: 70 in each serving

350 g (12 oz) white cabbage
425 g (15 oz) pineapple

canned in its own juice
Chopped mint – optional

Chop the cabbage finely – one of those spring-loaded round choppers is good for this – and put it into a bowl. Chop the pineapple and add it to the cabbage, together with the juice and the mint if you've got any. Mix together and serve as soon as possible.

CABBAGE, RED PEPPER AND CARROT

This is a pretty mixture: white cabbage with red pepper, orange carrot, green spring onions. It's best made with an olive oil dressing, but if you want to reduce the calories you can use some fat-free bottled dressing.

Serves 4
Calories: 85 in each serving

350 g (12 oz) white cabbage
1 carrot
1 red pepper
1 small bunch spring onions
25 g (1 oz) raisins or chopped
  dates

1 tablespoon good quality
  olive oil
1 tablespoon red wine vinegar
Salt and pepper

Chop the cabbage and put it into a large bowl. Scrape and grate the carrot, de-seed and slice the pepper, trim and chop the spring onions. Add all these to the cabbage, together with the raisins or chopped dates, the oil, vinegar and some salt and pepper. Mix well.

CARROT, APPLE, CELERY AND RAISIN

Orange juice makes a delicious dressing for this salad which is moist, sweet and crunchy.

Serves 4
Calories: 70 in each serving

1 head of celery
225 g (8 oz) carrots
2 large eating apples –
  Russets are particularly
  good

25 g (1 oz) raisins
About 75 ml (3 fl oz) orange
  juice

129

Wash and slice the celery; grate the carrot; dice the apples, removing the core. Put the celery, carrot, apple and raisins into a bowl and stir in the orange juice. Mix well. Serve as soon as possible.

CELERY AND CUCUMBER SALAD

This is a nice quick salad to make and lovely with pasta and rice dishes. You could use fennel instead of celery for a change.

Serves 4
Calories: 15 in each serving

1 good-sized head of celery
   (or 1–2 heads fennel)
1 cucumber

Salt and pepper
1 tablespoon lemon juice

Slice the celery; dice the cucumber. Mix them together, add salt and pepper to taste and the lemon juice.

CHICORY AND WATERCRESS

White chicory, with its crisp juicy texture and fresh flavour, makes a delicious salad and is quick to prepare. I like it mixed with watercress for flavour and colour contrast – and if you want to expand this salad even more, try putting it out on a serving plate with a pile of bright orange grated carrot in the centre, moistened with orange juice.

Serves 4
Calories: 30 with low-fat dressing; 90 with oil dressing, in each serving

350 g (12 oz) chicory
1 bunch watercress
3–4 tablespoons low-fat
   French dressing or

2 tablespoons olive oil and
  1 tablespoon wine vinegar
Sea salt and freshly ground
   black pepper

Separate the leaves of the chicory, wash and dry them. Wash the watercress, removing coarse stems and any damaged leaves. Put the chicory and watercress into a bowl and add the dressing or the oil, vinegar and a little seasoning. Turn the salad with a spoon so that it all gets lightly coated with dressing. Serve as soon as possible.

CUCUMBER, APPLE AND RAISIN SALAD

A friend of mine had this salad at, of all places, a motorway restaurant. It sounded good so I tried making a low-calorie version and it is a pleasant, easy-to-make combination.

Serves 4
Calories: 100 in each serving

1 cucumber	1 teaspoon olive oil
2 large eating apples	A drop of wine vinegar
1 tablespoon natural yoghurt	Sea salt and pepper
50 g (2 oz) curd cheese	50 g (2 oz) raisins

Dice the cucumber and apples, discarding the apple cores. Put the yoghurt, curd cheese and oil into a large bowl and beat until creamy, then add just a dash of vinegar and some salt and pepper to taste. Mix in the cucumber, apple and raisins.

CUCUMBER AND GREEN PEPPER

An easy-to-make salad, and the mixture of greens is pretty.

Serves 4
Calories: 90 in each serving

1 large cucumber	Sea salt and freshly ground
1 green pepper	black pepper
2 tablespoons olive oil	A little fresh or dried dill
1 tablespoon wine vinegar	weed if available

Slice the cucumber; slice and de-seed the pepper. Mix the cucumber and pepper slices in a bowl and add the oil, vinegar, a little salt and pepper and the dill if you're using it.

LETTUCE, CUCUMBER AND MINT

A crisp lettuce such as Webbs or Iceberg is best for this salad. Most of the calories come from the oil in the dressing: you could reduce them to a minimum by using just the lemon juice if you prefer.

Serves 4
Calories: 85 in each serving

1 crisp lettuce	2 tablespoons olive oil
1 cucumber	1 tablespoon lemon juice
1 onion, peeled	Sea salt and freshly ground
Chopped mint	black pepper

Break up the lettuce and put it into a bowl. Dice the cucumber and slice the onion; add these to the bowl, along with the mint, oil, lemon juice and a little salt and pepper as necessary. Turn the salad gently.

POTATO SALAD

This is a useful extra for serving with a salad main course if you want to make it more substantial. Although the dressing tastes creamy, it's not too rich and high in calories and the slight sharpness of the yoghurt makes it refreshing. The potatoes really do taste better if you cook them in their skins and then peel them and it doesn't take any longer – in fact I don't think it takes as much time as peeling them first.

Serves 4–6
Calories: 170 in each serving if serving 4; 110 if serving 6

450 g (1 lb) medium-sized
  potatoes – or new potatoes
  are lovely when available
Sea salt
2 tablespoons natural yoghurt

125 g (4 oz) curd cheese
2 teaspoons olive oil
½ teaspoon wine vinegar
Freshly ground black pepper

Put the potatoes into a saucepan, cover them with cold water and
add a little salt. Bring to the boil and simmer for about 20
minutes, until the potatoes are tender. Drain and cover them with
cold water. With a sharp, pointed knife, slip the skins off the
potatoes. Dice the potatoes. Put the yoghurt, curd cheese, oil and
vinegar into a bowl and beat together. Season well. Gently fold
in the potatoes. Cool before serving.

TOMATO AND ONION SALAD

You really do need firm, almost under-ripe tomatoes for this
salad, and the skins can be left on, or removed, according to taste.

Serves 4
Calories: 60 in each serving

700 g (1½ lb) tomatoes
1 onion, peeled
1 tablespoon olive oil
1 tablespoon red wine vinegar
Sea salt and freshly ground
  black pepper

Chopped fresh green herbs as
  available – basil is lovely if
  you can get it

Slice the tomatoes and onion and put them into a bowl. Add the
oil, vinegar, seasoning and the herbs and gently mix everything
together.

TOMATO AND WATERCRESS SALAD

A juicy and refreshing salad that's quick to make.

Serves 4
Calories: 75 in each serving

350 g (12 oz) firm tomatoes
1 bunch watercress
2 tablespoons best quality
  olive oil

1 tablespoon wine vinegar
Sea salt and freshly ground
  black pepper

Slice the tomatoes – which can be peeled first, or not, according to taste – and put them into a salad bowl. Wash the watercress and dry it in a clean tea cloth or a salad shaker. Add to the bowl, together with the oil, vinegar and a little seasoning. Turn the salad so that it all gets lightly coated with the oil and vinegar. Serve as soon as possible.

WATERCRESS, LETTUCE AND CELERY SALAD

A green salad that's useful almost all the year round. In the summer you can use cucumber instead of the celery and fresh herbs and a few very well washed dandelion leaves.

Serves 4
Calories: 80 in each serving

1 bunch of watercress
1 small lettuce
1 celery head
1 onion, peeled and sliced
2 tablespoons best quality
  olive oil

1 tablespoon wine vinegar
Sea salt and freshly ground
  black pepper

Wash the watercress, lettuce and celery and shake them dry. Put the watercress and lettuce into a salad bowl, breaking up the leaves as necessary. Slice the celery and add to the bowl, together with the onion, oil, vinegar and some salt and pepper. Mix everything lightly together and serve at once.

CARROT AND LEMON PURÉE

A vegetable purée is useful because it can take the place of both a cooked vegetable and a sauce or gravy. It also contrasts well with crisp dishes.

Serves 4
Calories: 90 in each serving

450 g (1 lb) carrots, scraped
225 g (½ lb) potatoes,
  peeled
7 g (¼ oz) margarine

Grated rind and juice of 1
  lemon
Sea salt and freshly ground
  black pepper

Cut the carrots and potatoes into even-sized pieces and cook them together in boiling water until tender. Drain, saving the water. Put the vegetables into the liquidizer with the margarine and 150 ml (¼ pint) of the reserved water and blend to a purée. Put the purée back into the saucepan and reheat. Just before serving add enough of the lemon to give a pleasant tang but don't let the mixture get too hot after this or it might taste slightly bitter. Season.

TO FREEZE: cool, freeze in a suitable container. To use, thaw completely and heat gently, stirring often.

CELERIAC AND POTATO PURÉE

Make as above, using 450 g (1 lb) celeriac and 225 g (8 oz) potatoes but leaving out the lemon. It's nice with 2 tablespoonfuls of fromage blanc swirled in just before serving, and some chopped parsley over the top.

Calories: 90 in each serving, 100 with fromage blanc

TO FREEZE: as above.

BAKED POTATOES

Potatoes in their jackets, baked in the oven, are about the most labour-saving vegetable to prepare and one of the most nutritious, if you eat the skins.

There are two ways of cooking jacket potatoes. If you want really crisp skins, wash the potatoes and put them on to a baking tin while they are still wet. Don't add any oil. Bake in a hot oven, 230°C (450°F), gas mark 8, for 1–1¼ hours, until the skins of the potatoes are very crisp and the inside feels soft when you squeeze the potato. The important thing here is to serve the potatoes as soon as they are done, and don't try to keep them in a lower oven or they will not be pleasant.

For potatoes which you want to be able to keep warm for longer you need to make the soft-skinned type of baked potato. Here you rub the skins lightly with just a little oil and bake the potatoes as above but you can reduce the oven temperature to 200°C (400°F), gas mark 6, after 30 minutes and bake for about 1–1¼ hours all together. Or start them off at the lower temperature and bake them for longer. They will also bake slowly at 160°C (325°F), gas mark 3, but you need to allow 2–3 hours. This is handy if you want to serve the potatoes with a casserole or want to leave them to cook while you're out.

BIRCHER POTATOES

This potato dish was the idea of Dr Bircher Benner, who also invented muesli. I think it's a very good way of cooking potatoes because it combines the advantages of both baked and roast potatoes without much fat.

Calories: about 165 for a 175 g (6 oz) potato

1 medium-sized potato per person   A very little oil

Set the oven to 200°C (400°F), gas mark 6. Scrub the potato or potatoes and cut in half lengthwise, or into chunks, as for roast potatoes. Brush the cut surfaces of the potato with oil and place on a very lightly oiled baking tin. Bake for about 35–45 minutes, until the halves feel tender and the cut sides are golden brown and crisp, like good roast potatoes.

MASHED POTATOES

Light, creamy mashed potatoes are delicious, but be careful not to add too much fat. Use just a little polyunsaturated margarine (7 g [¼ oz]) and some liquid skimmed milk to mash 700 g (1½ lb) potatoes, season carefully and beat really well until light and fluffy.

Serves 4–6
Calories: about 170 if serving 4; 115 if serving 6

NEW POTATOES

I must say I think you need some margarine or butter with the first new potatoes, but they are also good if you boil and drain them then stir in a couple of tablespoonfuls of fromage blanc and some chopped chives, spring onions or dill.

Calories: 110 a serving if using 450 g (1 lb) potatoes, 2 tablespoons fromage blanc and serving 4 people

---

ROAST POTATOES

Crisp golden roast potatoes needn't be as fatty as many people think. I have carefully measured both the amount of oil I put into

137

the tin and the amount left at the end and find that the difference is only 2 tablespoonfuls if you do the potatoes this way.

Serves 4
Calories: 205 in each serving

700 g (1½ lb) potatoes
Sunflower or corn oil

Set the oven to 230°C (450°F), gas mark 8. Peel the potatoes and cut them in halves or quarters. Par-boil them for 5 minutes. While the potatoes are boiling pour enough oil into a roasting tin to just cover the surface – don't make it deeper than 3 mm (⅛ in). Put the tin into the oven to heat.

The potatoes and the oil must both be hot. So drain the potatoes then take the tin of oil out of the oven and put it on the hot plate or gas flame on top of your cooker while you tip the potatoes into the oil – stand back because there will be a sizzling and a spluttering. Turn the potatoes in the oil then quickly put the tin back into the oven and bake for 45–60 minutes, turning them after about 30 minutes. Drain well on kitchen paper and serve immediately.

Puddings

When you're watching your fat and sugar intake you might think that puddings would be a problem. In fact it is surprising how many really delicious ones you can make using fresh and dried fruits, yoghurt, low-fat white cheese and just a little honey for sweetening.

With these ingredients you can make luscious fools, creamy, authentic-tasting ice creams, fruit salads and compotes, smooth cheesecake, and you can serve them with rich toppings which are low in fat and calories – I've given recipes for these in the icings, fillings, creams and toppings section. So you see you don't have to give up lovely puddings in order to be healthy!

BAKED APPLES WITH RAISINS

Serves 4
Calories: 90 in each serving

4 large cooking apples
50 g (2 oz) raisins

Wash the apples and remove cores, using an apple corer or by cutting them out neatly with a sharp pointed knife. Score round the middle of the apples, just cutting the skin. Place the apples in a shallow ovenproof dish. Fill the cavities of the apples with raisins, pressing them down well. Bake the apples, uncovered, at 180°C (350°F), mark 4, for 45–60 minutes, until the apples are tender.

These are nice served just as they are, or with natural yoghurt or one of the low-fat toppings. Other fillings can be used instead

139

of the raisins; dates are good and so is a spoonful of the healthy mincemeat in the preserves section.

TO FREEZE: unsuitable.

APPLE, DATE AND ORANGE COMPOTE

The dates in this recipe provide a natural sweetness and the orange gives a pleasant tang. It's good with a dollop of icy cold fromage blanc or one of the pouring toppings.

Serves 4
Calories: 145 in each serving

700 g (1½ lb) cooking apples   1 orange
125 g (4 oz) cooking dates

Peel, core and slice the apples; cut the dates into small pieces, discarding any stones. Scrub the orange in hot water to remove any residue of sprays, then finely grate or pare off thin strips of peel. Squeeze the juice from the orange. Put the apples and dates into a saucepan and add the orange juice. Cover and simmer gently until the apples and dates are tender – 10–15 minutes. Serve hot or cold, with the slivers of peel sprinkled on top.

TO FREEZE: cool, put into a suitable container, label and freeze. To use, allow to defrost, then heat gently.

WHOLEWHEAT APPLE PIE

If you want to keep your day's eating fairly low in fat, you've got to plan a meal carefully if you want to serve a pie, whether it's a savoury one or a sweet one. But it is perfectly possible to do this and then a fruit pie makes a lovely treat. The wholewheat pastry gives a delicious nutty flavour.

Serves 6–8
Calories: 350 a portion if serving 6; 265 if serving 8

200 g (8 oz) wholewheat flour   450 g (1 lb) cooking apples
100 g (4 oz) polyunsaturated   125 g (4 oz) raisins, chopped
  margarine   cooking dates or sultanas
2 tablespoons cold water

First make the pastry. Sift the flour into a large bowl, adding the residue of bran left in the sieve (the reason for sieving is to aerate the flour and when this has been done the bran can be put back). Add the fat and use a fork to blend it lightly into the flour. When the mixture looks like rather coarse breadcrumbs stir in the water and form into a dough. Leave on one side to rest while you prepare the apples by peeling and slicing them, discarding the cores.

Set the oven to 220°C (425 F), gas mark 7. Roll out two-thirds of the pastry and use to line a pie dish. Put in the apples and then the raisins, dates or sultanas. Roll out the remaining pastry and use this to cover the pie, trimming the edges neatly and decorating the top with the re-rolled trimmings if you like. Prick the top of the pie then bake it in the oven for 30–35 minutes.

This pie is lovely with one of the hot sauces, such as the amond sauce, or with a pouring low-fat cream, all from the toppings section.

TO FREEZE: I prefer to part-bake this pie to cook the apple a little before freezing. Bake for 15–20 minutes, cool, open-freeze, then wrap. To use, allow the pie to thaw then bake for about 20 minutes.

APPLE SNOW

A delicious low-calorie pudding which is simplicity itself to make.

Serves 4
Calories: 70 in each serving

450 g (1 lb) cooking apples   2 egg whites
1 tablespoon clear honey   A little grated lemon rind

Peel, core and slice the apples then put them into a heavy-based saucepan with the honey and cook them over a gentle heat, with a lid on the saucepan, until they're soft and purée-like. If the apples have produced a great deal of liquid take the lid off the saucepan and cook them for a few minutes longer to thicken them up but watch them carefully and stir often so that they don't burn. Cool, then sieve or liquidize.

Whisk the egg whites until they're stiff but not dry then fold them into the apple purée. Grate enough lemon rind into the mixture to give a refreshing tang. Divide between four bowls and serve chilled.

TO FREEZE: unsuitable, although you could make the apple purée part and store that in the freezer.

APRICOT FOOL

This smooth, golden cream looks and tastes too rich and luxurious to be good for you – but it is! It's made from that favourite ingredient of mine, smooth low-fat white cheese – fromage blanc. If the apricots are nice and sweet they will provide all the sweetening necessary, otherwise you can use a little honey.

Serves 4
Calories: 175 in each serving, without extra sweetening, almonds or sesame seeds

175 g (6 oz) dried apricots   A few toasted flaked almonds
350 g (12 oz) fromage blanc   or sesame seeds
1 tablespoon honey – optional

Wash the apricots well in hot water. Put them into a medium-sized saucepan and cover with cold water. Leave to soak for an hour or so if possible, then simmer them over a low heat for 20–30 minutes, until they're very tender and the water is reduced to just a little syrupy glaze. (It's best if you have the time to let them soak first, but I have found that you can get away with just simmering them if you're rushed for time.) Cool, then liquidize to a thick purée. Mix the apricot purée with the fromage blanc, beating well until smooth and creamy and add honey if liked. Spoon the mixture into four dishes – it looks lovely in glass ones – and chill. Serve sprinkled with a few toasted flaked almonds or sesame seeds.

TO FREEZE: put mixture into a polythene container, label, store. To use, thaw completely then beat well before putting into individual glasses and garnishing with nuts.

CHRISTMAS PUDDING

This is a beautiful dark, glossy Christmas pudding which is sweet and spicy, even though it contains no sugar. It's my healthy, sugarless version of our traditional family pudding, but the dried fruits are so sweet in themselves that no one can tell the difference between this one and a 'normal' pudding! In fact it makes me wonder why we ever put sugar into Christmas puddings at all.

Makes 1 large pudding which serves 8–10 at least
Calories: 635 a portion if serving 8; 510 if serving 10

225 g (8 oz) cooking dates
150 ml (¼ pint) rum or milk
225 g (8 oz) polyunsaturated margarine
2 eggs, beaten
1 tablespoon black treacle
Grated rind and juice of 1 lemon
125 g (4 oz) stoned raisins, chopped
125 g (4 oz) whole candied peel, chopped

25 g (1 oz) blanched almonds, chopped
225 g (8 oz) currants
125 g (4 oz) sultanas
125 g (4 oz) plain wholewheat flour
125 g (4 oz) soft wholewheat breadcrumbs
½ teaspoon grated nutmeg
½ teaspoon ground ginger
1½ teaspoons mixed spice

Cut up the cooking dates, being careful to remove any stones

143

and hard pieces of stem. Put the dates into a small saucepan with the milk or rum and heat gently until mushy. Remove from heat and cool. Cream together the margarine and dates in a large mixing bowl, then beat in the eggs, treacle, lemon rind and juice. Add all the remaining ingredients, stirring well to make a soft mixture which will fall heavily from the spoon when shaken. Put the mixture into a well greased 900 ml (2 pint) pudding basin or two 550 ml (1 pint) basins, filling to 2 cm (1 in) from the top. Cover with greased greaseproof paper and piece of foil, tying down well. Steam for 4 hours, topping up the water with more boiling water as necessary. Store in a cool dry place; steam for another 3 hours before serving. It's lovely with the almond custard or one of the low-fat creams from the next section.

COFFEE ICE CREAM WITH MAPLE SYRUP AND WALNUTS

Although this doesn't contain any of the normal ingredients, it tastes and looks very much like a really good ice cream, smooth and velvety. The fromage blanc does give it a slightly sharp flavour, which may not be to everyone's taste, but I think it makes it more refreshing. If you don't like to use coffee, the ice cream could be flavoured with a little carob powder instead. I like to use maple syrup for the occasional treat and, like honey, I consider it to be preferable to sugar. But be careful to buy the real thing and not 'maple-flavoured syrup'. If you can't get maple syrup you could always use a couple of tablespoons of clear honey instead.

Serves 4–6
Calories: 305 a portion if serving 4; 200 if serving 6

500 g (1 lb 1 oz) fromage blanc
4 teaspoons 'continental' Nescafé

4 tablespoons maple syrup
50 g (2 oz) chopped mixed nuts

Turn the fridge to its coldest setting. Put the fromage blanc into a bowl and beat it with a fork until smooth. Dissolve the Nescafé

144

in the maple syrup in a small bowl or old cup and add to the fromage blanc, together with the nuts. Mix well. Spoon into a plastic container which will fit in the ice compartment of your fridge. Freeze the ice cream until firm. You don't have to stir this ice cream during freezing, but take it out of the fridge 20 or 30 minutes before the meal to give it a chance to soften up a bit and beat it before serving; it tastes best if it is not too frozen.

TO FREEZE: this ice cream will keep very well in a plastic container in the deep freeze. Allow 1 hour for it to unfreeze at room temperature and beat it before serving. If it gets a little soft just pop it back into the fridge for a 10 minutes or so – it won't spoil.

DATE FLAN WITH ORANGE PASTRY

The dates make a lovely moist sweet filling for this flan. Serve it warm with a dollop of chilled natural yoghurt, fromage blanc or one of the low-fat toppings; their smooth cool sharpness provides a perfect contrast to the sweet crunchy pie.

Serves 6–8
Calories: 385 a portion if serving 6; 290 if serving 8

225 g (8 oz) cooking dates
150 ml ($\frac{1}{4}$ pint) orange juice
200 g (8 oz) wholewheat flour

100 g (4 oz) polyunsaturated margarine
Grated rind of 1 orange and 2 tablespoons of the juice

Chop the dates coarsely, removing any stones or hard bits. Put the dates into a small saucepan with the orange juice and heat gently until mushy. Cool.

Make the pastry; sift the flour into a bowl, adding also the residue of bran from the sieve. Using a fork, mix in the margarine, orange rind and the 2 tablespoons orange juice to make a dough. Roll out the dough and use to line a 22 cm (8 in) flan dish; spoon in the date mixture, smoothing it level with the back of the spoon. Trim the pastry. Re-roll the trimmings and cut into

145

thin strips; arrange these in a lattice on top of the tart. Bake the tart in the oven for 30 minutes. Serve hot, or warm.

TO FREEZE: open-freeze after baking; wrap in polythene. To use, thaw, then heat through in a cool oven.

FRUIT COMPOTE IN GINGER WINE

You can buy dried fruit salad mixture at health shops and in some supermarkets and it makes a lovely pudding, especially if you stew it and then marinade it in ginger wine, as in this recipe. (An alternative, if you don't want to use the wine, is to add some ground ginger or chopped crystallized ginger to the water.) Top it with a generous dollop of one of the slightly sharp-tasting low-fat creams for a delicious blend of flavours and textures.

Serves 4–6
Calories: 300 a portion if serving 4; 200 if serving 6

450 g (1 lb) mixed dried fruit salad – apricots, peaches, pears, prunes and apple rings	Water to cover 150 ml ($\frac{1}{4}$ pint) green ginger wine

Put the dried fruit into a medium-sized saucepan, cover generously with cold water and if possible leave to soak for a couple of hours or so. Then simmer the fruit over a gentle heat, without a lid on the saucepan, for about 30 minutes, until it is very tender and the liquid has reduced to just a little glossy-looking syrup. Remove from the heat and pour in the wine. Leave to cool, then chill before serving. It looks good in a pretty glass bowl, or in individual glasses, topped with a swirl of low-fat cream.

TO FREEZE: freeze in a polythene container; to use, thaw and serve.

GREEN FRUIT SALAD

Kiwi fruit – those little egg-shaped furry brown fruits – look so beautiful when they're sliced, with their vivid green flesh and flower-like centre and I wanted to serve them in a way that would really show them off. That's how I got the idea for this fruit salad which is made entirely of green fruits – pale green melon, green grapes, greengages if you can get them, and of course the kiwi fruit.

Serves 6
Calories: 85 in each portion

1 small melon with green flesh – honeydew, ogen or gallia
225 g (8 oz) green grapes
225 g (8 oz) greengages – or use some extra grapes and kiwi fruits
2 kiwi fruits
150 ml ($\frac{1}{4}$ pint) apple juice

Halve the melon and remove the seeds. Scoop out or dice the flesh neatly. Put the melon pieces into a large bowl. Wash, halve and de-seed the grapes; halve and stone the greengages. Peel the kiwi fruits with a sharp knife and slice them into thin rounds. Add these fruits to the melon, together with the apple juice. Transfer to a pretty bowl to serve.

TO FREEZE: unsuitable.

RASPBERRY CREAMS

This is an almost instant pudding that tastes creamy and delicious. Even the best quality fruit yoghurt contains some sugar (see page 9), but if you like fruit yoghurt, mixing it with some low-calorie white cheese means you get less sugar in each portion. It's particularly good if you can chill it before serving.

Serves 4
Calories: 145 in each serving

225 g (8 oz) fromage blanc
2 200 g (7 oz) raspberry
  yoghurts, preferably a real
  fruit variety without artifical
  colouring or flavouring

Put the fromage blanc and the yoghurt into a bowl and mix together. Spoon into four dishes and, if possible, chill thoroughly before serving.

SUMMER FRUIT SALAD

Apricots, peaches and strawberries, soaked in orange juice (to which you can add a dash of orange liqueur, if you like, for special occasions) and chilled make a luscious fruit salad. I can't think of a nicer pudding for a hot summer's day.

Serves 4
Calories: 60 in each serving, without liqueur; 80 with liqueur

225 g (8 oz) ripe apricots
2–3 ripe peaches
225 g (8 oz) strawberries
150 ml (¼ pint) orange juice
Thinly pared rind from
  ½ orange

1–2 tablespoons cointreau or
  other orange liqueur –
  optional

Wash the apricots and peaches, halve and remove stones. Slice flesh fairly thinly. Wash and hull the strawberries; halve or quarter any large ones so that they are all about the same size. Put all the fruits into a pretty bowl and pour in the orange juice. Snip the rind into thin slivers and add these to the fruit, together with the liqueur if you're using it. Chill for 1 hour or so before serving if possible.

TO FREEZE: unsuitable.

WINTER FRUIT SALAD

Winter is really quite a good time for making a fruit salad; there are usually some lovely sweet pineapples and pears around, as well as those firm green grapes; oranges are juicy and good and there's a choice of apples. My favourites for this salad are Russets or Cox.

Serves 4–6
Calories: 80 in each portion if serving 6; 100 if serving 4

½ large or 1 small ripe sweet pineapple
2 oranges
1 large Russet or Cox apple

1 ripe pear
125 g (4 oz) green grapes
150 ml (¼ pint) orange juice

Cut the leafy green top and prickly skin from the pineapple and trim away any little prickly tufts that remain. Dice the flesh, discarding any hard core. Put the pieces into a large bowl. Holding the oranges over the bowl and using a sharp knife, cut the skin and pith from them, then cut the segments out of the inner skin. Squeeze this skin over the bowl to extract any remaining juice. Peel the apple and pear if necessary; cut flesh into pieces, removing core. Halve and de-seed the grapes. Add to the bowl, together with the orange juice. Chill before serving.

TO FREEZE: unsuitable.

TROPICAL FRUIT SALAD

If you can get a fresh ripe mango, it makes a lovely addition to this salad; it should feel slightly soft to the touch. The powdered cardamom gives this salad a subtly exotic, almost perfumed flavour which we think is delicious, but you can of course leave it out if you prefer.

Serves 4
Calories: 112 in each serving

½ small ripe pineapple
2 oranges
1 banana
1 kiwi fruit

1 ripe mango
1–2 teaspoons powdered
cardamom
150 ml (¼ pint) orange juice

Cut the leafy top and prickly skin from the pineapple, then use the point of the knife to scoop out any little prickly tufts that remain. Dice the flesh, cutting away and discarding any hard core. Put the pieces in a large bowl. Hold the oranges over the bowl and cut away the skin with a sharp knife, round and round, like peeling an apple. Then cut out the segments one by one and add them to the bowl. Squeeze the remains of the orange over the bowl to extract the last of the juice. Peel and slice the banana and kiwi fruit. Using a sharp knife, cut the peel from the mango and then slice off little pieces of the flesh until you come to the big stone in the middle. Add the mango to the other fruit and pour in the orange juice. Sprinkle over the powdered cardamom. Mix well. Chill before serving.

TO FREEZE: unsuitable.

GINGER SYLLABUB

This healthy version of a syllabub is made from fromage blanc, that beautifully creamy white cheese that's low in calories but which, I think, tastes as rich and good as cream. It has a slightly sharp taste, rather like the French *crème fraîche*, which makes it very refreshing. If you'd prefer not to use wine, make this syllabub with 4 tablespoons natural yoghurt and ½ teaspoon ground ginger instead.

Serves 4–6
Calories: 275 a portion if serving 4; 185 if serving 6

500 g (1 lb 1 oz) fromage blanc
4 tablespoons clear honey or
maple syrup
4 tablespoons ginger wine

4 pieces preserved stem ginger
finely chopped, about 75 g
(3 oz) in all

Put the fromage blanc into a large bowl and beat with a fork until smooth, then stir in the rest of the ingredients. Spoon mixture into individual glasses or small dishes and chill well before serving.

TO FREEZE: freeze in a polythene container. To use, thaw, then beat until light and creamy.

HONEY CHEESECAKE

A smooth cheesecake makes one of the most luscious desserts and I'm pleased with this one because it has a crisp base and thick, firm layer of rich, creamy topping yet is surprisingly low in calories and fat – so you can eat it with a clear conscience. I think it looks attractive topped with a shiny glaze of sugarless jam or some fresh orange segments.

Serves 10–12
Calories: 290 a portion if serving 10; 230 if serving 12

125 g (4 oz) Grapenuts or wholewheat biscuit crumbs
40 g (1½ oz) margarine
2 teaspoons honey

500 g (1 lb 1 oz) quark
3 tablespoons honey
2 eggs
1 teaspoon vanilla extract

For the topping:
350 g (12 oz) sugarless jam, preferably damson or apricot

You really need one of those snap-ring tins so that you can take the cheesecake out easily, but if you haven't got one, press a large piece of foil into an 18 cm (7 in) cake tin so that it covers the base and sides, then you will be able to lift the cheesecake out easily.

Set the oven to 190°C (375°F), gas mark 5. Mix together the Grapenuts or crumbs, margarine and honey; press over the base of the tin. Put the fromage blanc into a bowl and beat with a fork, then mix in the honey, eggs and vanilla, to make a smooth cream. Spoon this into the tin, spreading it carefully over the base.

Level the top with a knife, then bake for 40–60 minutes, until firm. Cool, then glaze the top by melting the jam and pouring quickly over the cheesecake. Serve chilled and use a sharp knife to cut it.

TO FREEZE: cook the cheesecake then cool. Open-freeze, wrap carefully, label. To use, loosen wrappings and allow to defrost completely.

HONEY MUESLI

This is a moist, creamy muesli, flavoured with honey and topped with crunchy nuts. I like it especially when it's made with mellow Bramley apples which have been stored for a couple of months, but it can be made with any firm, not-too-sweet apple.

Serves 4
Calories: 310 in each serving – you can reduce the calories to 230 a portion if you leave out the nuts

4 large apples
150 ml (¼ pint) natural yoghurt
50 g (2 oz) rolled oats
50 g (2 oz) barley flakes – from health shops, but if you can't get them use extra rolled oats instead
1 tablespoon clear honey
25–50 g (1–2 oz) raisins
75 g (3 oz) chopped hazel nuts

Peel and coarsely grate the apple. Put into a large bowl and stir in the yoghurt, oats, barley, honey, raisins and two-thirds of the nuts. Mix well, then spoon into four serving bowls. Sprinkle the nuts on top and serve as soon as possible.

TO FREEZE: unsuitable.

ORANGE AND ALMOND ICE CREAM

This is a smooth, creamy golden ice. It's ridiculously easy to make, healthy and extremely popular with everyone who tries it. It's superb in the summer with small sweet ripe stawberries, and for a dinner partly studded with vivid green pistachio nuts instead of the almonds.

Serves 6–8
Calories: 180 a portion if serving 6, 135 if serving 8

500 g (1 lb 1 oz) fromage blanc
½ 170 ml (6 fl oz) carton frozen concentrated orange
2 tablespoons clear honey

40 g (1½ oz) flaked almonds, toasted under a moderate grill for a few minutes until golden

Turn the fridge to its coldest setting. Put the fromage blanc into a bowl and beat in the orange and honey. Mix well until smooth and creamy. Pour into a plastic container which will fit the freezing part of your fridge and freeze until solid. Take the ice cream out of the fridge 30 minutes before the meal, then beat it before serving – it tastes best if it's not too hard – and stir in the almonds.

TO FREEZE: this freezes well but allow time for the ice cream to soften before serving.

FRESH ORANGE SALAD

Fresh oranges make a pudding that's very refreshing and healthy as well as delicious. Yet usually they're served covered in a thick syrup which spoils them from the health point of view and isn't necessary if you use really sweet oranges. A tablespoonful of orange liqueur makes a lovely addition, though, for a special occasion.

Serves 4–6
Calories: 90 a portion if serving 4; 60 if serving 6, without liqueur, which adds about 20 calories a portion

6 large oranges
150 ml (¼ pint) orange juice

2 tablespoons orange liqueur such as cointreau – optional

153

Scrub one of the oranges under hot water and cut off some thin strips of peel using a potato peeler. Snip the peel into fine shreds and leave on one side. Cut the peel and pith from the oranges, holding them over a bowl as you do so to catch any juice. Then cut the segments away from the inner skin and put them into the bowl. Squeeze the remaining skin over the bowl to extract any extra juice. Add the 150 ml ($\frac{1}{4}$ pint) orange juice to the oranges in the bowl, also the reserved shreds of peel and the liqueur if you're using it. Chill thoroughly before serving.

PANCAKES WITH MAPLE SYRUP

Although you might think of pancakes as being greasy, they're not because they're only cooked in a very little oil. They therefore make a good, substantial pudding and one that's always popular with my children. If I've got time I like to make a double batch, wrap half in foil and keep them in the freezer. They can be heated through in a moderate oven and make a useful weekend pudding when life is hectic.

Makes 12 pancakes
Calories: about 70 a pancake, without maple syrup.

125 g (4 oz) wholewheat flour   Oil for frying
2 eggs   Maple syrup (or clear
1 tablespoon oil   honey), slices of lemon
200 ml (8 fl oz) liquid
  skimmed milk

If you've got a liquidizer, simply put the flour, eggs, oil and milk into the goblet and blend until smooth. Otherwise put the flour into a bowl, break in the eggs and add the oil and milk gradually, beating to a smooth consistency. If you're making the batter ahead of time, leave it to stand, but if not, don't worry as it doesn't seem to make much difference, especially if you use the liquidizer method.

Brush a small frying pan with oil and set over a moderate heat. When hot, put in two tablespoonfuls or so of the batter.

Tip and swirl the frying pan so that the batter runs all over the base and covers it thinly. When the top has set, use a spatula and your fingers to flip the pancake over and cook the other side, which will do very quickly. Remove from the frying pan and put on to a plate. Cover with foil and keep warm in a low oven while you make the rest. Serve the pancakes with maple syrup and slices of lemon.

TO FREEZE: just wrap the pile of pancakes in foil, label and freeze. There is no need to put pieces of greaseproof paper between them. To use, loosen the foil, thaw or half thaw and put the package in a slow oven to de-frost and heat through.

PEACHES IN WHITE WINE

This is a simple yet very delicious pudding. Make it in the summer when peaches are cheap and good. You can also make this successfully using red grape juice instead of wine.

Serves 6
Calories: 90 in each serving

6 ripe peaches   2 teaspoons honey
300 ml ($\frac{1}{2}$ pint) sweet white
   wine

Put the peaches into a bowl and cover with boiling water. Leave for 1 minute, then drain. Remove the skins with a sharp knife and cut the peaches into thin slices, discarding the stones. Put the slices into a glass serving bowl. Mix the wine with the honey and pour over the peaches. Chill before serving.

TO FREEZE: unsuitable.

PINEAPPLE AND ORANGE COMPOTE

A really ripe, juicy pineapple makes a lovely, refreshing pudding.

Serves 4
Calories: 75 in each portion

1 ripe pineapple
150 ml (¼ pint) orange juice

Cut leaves and skin from pineapple and scoop out the prickly tufts with the point of a knife. Dice flesh, discarding any tough core. Put the pineapple into a bowl – a glass one looks pretty – and stir in the orange juice. Chill before serving.

TO FREEZE: unsuitable.

RAISIN AND NUT FLAN WITH SPICY PASTRY

This is a lovely flan, crisp cinnamon-flavoured pastry filled with a moist, lightly spiced mixture of raisins and creamy cheese. I find the pastry keeps crisp even after the flan has been in the fridge overnight. It's quick to make as the filling is uncooked.

Serves 8
Calories: 310 in each serving

150 g (6 oz) raisins
150 g (6 oz) wholewheat flour
½ teaspoon allspice or ground cloves
1 teaspoon ground cinnamon
75 g (3 oz) polyunsaturated margarine

1 tablespoon cold water
250 g (8¾ oz) quark
2–3 tablespoons liquid skimmed milk
1 teaspoon thick honey
50 g (2 oz) flaked almonds

Set the oven to 200°C (400°F), gas mark 6. Put the raisins into a small bowl and cover with boiling water. Leave for 10 minutes to plump, then drain. Meanwhile make the pastry. Sift the flour, allspice and half the cinnamon into a bowl, adding also the residue of bran left in the sieve. Using a fork blend in the margarine until the mixture looks like coarse breadcrumbs then add the water and mix to a dough. Roll out on a lightly floured board and use to line a 20 cm (8 in) flan dish. Prick the pastry all over then bake in the oven for 15 minutes, until lightly browned and crisp. Leave to cool while you make the filling.

Mix together the quark, raisins, skimmed milk and remaining half a teaspoonful of cinnamon. When it's creamy, stir in half the nuts. Spoon the filling into the cooked flan case and smooth the top. Sprinkle with a little more cinnamon and the remaining almonds. Chill before serving – it will get firmer, but you will need a sharp knife to cut it cleanly.

TO FREEZE: unsuitable.

YOGHURT

You can certainly save money if you make your own yoghurt and it is really very easy to do. I find I need to buy a fresh pot every three or four times I make it, otherwise I just save a little from the previous batch to start the next. When you're making yoghurt you can make a very simple pudding by putting some of the mixture into those little individual ramekins: it will set beautifully and get firm as it chills. Then all you have to do is top it with some maple syrup, clear honey, chopped nuts, Jordan's original crunchy, preserved ginger or sugar free jam before serving.

Makes 575 ml (1 pint)
Calories: 15 calories in 25 ml (1 fl oz)

575 ml (1 pint) liquid skimmed milk
2 rounded tablespoons skimmed milk powder

1 teaspoon fresh natural yoghurt – from a carton or from your last batch

Put the milk into a saucepan and bring up to the boil, then leave to simmer gently without a lid for 10 minutes. This reduces the milk slightly and helps to make the yoghurt thick and creamy. Remove the saucepan from the heat and leave until the milk is luke-warm. Meanwhile wash a couple of jars and sterilize them by swishing them out with warm water with some household bleach added, then rinse thoroughly in hot water.

Whisk the skimmed milk powder and the yoghurt into the milk then pour it into your clean jars, cover with foil and leave in a warm place for a few hours or overnight until it's firm. By the pilot light on a gas cooker is a good place, or in an airing cupboard. Cool the yoghurt, then put it into the fridge to chill and firm up.

TO FREEZE: unsuitable.

YOGHURT GLORY

If you like yoghurt, this is a mouthwatering way of serving it in a tall glass to look like a pink and white striped knickerbocker glory. It looks far more calorific than it really is and makes a good treat for slimmers.

Serves 2
Calories: 140 in each serving

1 medium-sized banana
125 ml (4 fl oz) raspberry, blackcurrant or strawberry yoghurt – preferably without artificial flavouring or colouring

125 ml (4 fl oz) low-fat natural yoghurt
15 g ($\frac{1}{2}$ oz) toasted hazel nuts, chopped

Peel the banana and slice thinly. Spoon a little of the flavoured yoghurt into the base of two tall glasses, then add some banana slices. Top with a layer of natural yoghurt followed by more of the fruit yoghurt. Continue in this way until all the ingredients are used up. Sprinkle the nuts on top and serve at once.

TO FREEZE: unsuitable.

Cakes and Biscuits

Although one may have reservations about the health aspect of cakes and biscuits, I think there will probably always be some occasions for them and it's rewarding to be able to make ones which are as healthy as possible.

One advantage of making your own cakes and biscuits is that at least you know what they've got in them. If you choose your ingredients carefully you can avoid all the antioxidants, bleaching agents, colourings, flavourings and preservatives commonly added to manufactured cakes. You can also make your home-made cakes doubly healthy by using wholewheat flour and polyunsaturated margarine and by reducing the amount of sugar or even cutting it out all together.

All the cakes and biscuits in this book are made without sugar. For some I have just used the natural sweetness of dried fruit and in others I've used honey, both of which I consider to be healthier than either white or brown sugar.

Making cakes without sugar is quite a challenge but it is surprising what you can do and I had great fun experimenting. I hope you will enjoy the results.

CHOCOLATE AND HONEY CAKE

You can bake this cake in one deep tin or two sandwich tins and either way it always comes out light and delectable. It can be served as it is or filled and spread with any of the sugarless toppings in the next section. If you are very health conscious and don't like to use any chocolate because of the caffeine which it contains, you could use carob powder from the health shop instead.

Makes 1 18–20 cm (7–8 in) cake
Calories: 290 in one slice (one-tenth of cake) without filling

175 g (6 oz) soft
  polyunsaturated margarine
175 g (6 oz) clear honey
2 large eggs
1 teaspoon extract of vanilla

225 g (8 oz) plain wholewheat
  flour
3 teaspoons baking powder
25 g (1 oz) cocoa

Line the base and sides of a deep 20 cm (8 in) cake tin with greaseproof paper or, if you're using two 18 cm (7 in) sandwich tins, just line them with a circle of greaseproof and brush the sides lightly with butter. Set the oven to 160°C (325°F), gas mark 3.

Put the margarine, honey, eggs and vanilla into a large bowl or the bowl of an electric mixer and sift the flour, baking powder and cocoa on top, adding also the residue of bran from the sieve. Beat everything together until light and thick and creamy: this takes around 3 minutes with an electric beater, about 5 minutes with a wooden spoon.

Spoon the mixture into the tin or tins, gently levelling the top, and bake for 25–30 minutes for sandwich cakes, or 1–1¼ hours for one deeper cake – the cake should spring back when pressed lightly in the middle with a fingertip. Cool on a wire rack, then fill and ice with one of the toppings from the next section.

TO FREEZE: see below.

CHOCOLATE BUNS

You can also use this mixture to make little buns: I think these come out best if you use paper cases, placed inside straight-sided bun tins for baking. Half the mixture above will make 24 buns and they take about 10 minutes at 160°C (325°F), gas mark 3. They are nice topped with a honey glaze (see next section) and some chopped nuts.

Calories: 60 in each bun, without topping or nuts

TO FREEZE: both the cake and the buns freeze well. Cool after baking then wrap in polythene and freeze. To use, unwrap, and allow to defrost at room temperature.

CHRISTMAS CAKE

There is no added sugar or honey in this cake; it is sweetened entirely by dried fruit yet, as I think you'll agree if you try it, it's certainly sweet and isn't at all strange either in taste or looks! It is lovely just as it is, but if you want to ice it – and my family certainly don't consider it to be a proper Christmas cake unless it is covered with almond paste and white icing – you can use the honey almond paste and fluffy white honey frosting in the toppings section. If you're very health conscious you may not approve of my using candied peel and glace cherries, but I like them for this once-a-year special cake. You could use chopped dried apricots and dates instead, though.

Makes 1 20 cm (8 in) round cake
Calories: about 90 for a 28 g (1 oz) piece, without almond paste and icing

175 g (6 oz) cooking dates, from a block
4 tablespoons water
175 g (6 oz) soft polyunsaturated margarine
5 eggs
175 g (6 oz) plain wholewheat flour
1 teaspoon mixed spice
75 g (3 oz) ground almonds

Grated rind and juice of 1 lemon
225 g (8 oz) currants
175 g (6 oz) raisins
175 g (6 oz) sultanas
125 g (4 oz) candied peel, chopped
125 g (4 oz) glace cherries
50 g (2 oz) flaked almonds
1–2 tablespoons brandy

Break up the dates with your fingers, being careful to remove any stones and hard pieces of stalk. Put the dates into a small saucepan with the water and stir over a moderate heat until mushy. Remove from the heat and cool. Set the oven to 150°C (300°F), gas mark 2. Line a 20 cm (8 in) cake tin with two layers of greaseproof paper and tie a piece of brown paper around the outside.

Put the cooled dates into a large bowl with the margarine and beat until light and creamy - like creaming fat and sugar together – then beat in the eggs, one by one. Sift in the flour and spice and beat again. Add all the remaining ingredients except the brandy and mix well together. Spoon the mixture into the prepared tin and bake in the oven for 4½–5 hours – a skewer should come out clean when pushed into the centre. Cool cake on a wire rack. When the cake is cold, remove the paper, prick the cake with a skewer and pour the brandy all over it.

TO FREEZE: although you can freeze this cake in the same way as the chocolate and honey cake, normally there seems little point as it keeps well in a tin.

DUNDEE CAKE

As with all the cakes in this book, there's no added sugar in this cake. All the sweetness comes from the dried fruit and either honey, or some extra dates, cooked into a pulp. I think the honey gives a slightly lighter result, but the dates work out cheaper, and are also very good, so you can take your pick. Whichever version you make, I don't expect anyone will realize that there's anything unusual about this cake unless you tell them. It's also good for Christmas, if you like a lighter type of cake.

Makes 1 18–20 cm (7–8 in) cake
Calories: 90 in a 28 g (1 oz) slice

175 g (6 oz) cooking dates (from a block) and 150 ml (5 fl oz) water, or 175 g (6 oz) clear honey
125 g (4 oz) soft polyunsaturated margarine
Grated rind of 1 lemon
3 eggs

225 g (8 oz) plain wholewheat flour
2 teaspoons baking powder
1 teaspoon mixed spice
450 g (1 lb) mixed dried fruit
25 g (1 oz) ground almonds
25 g (1 oz) flaked almonds, or split blanched almonds

Line the sides and base of an 18–20 cm (7–8 in) cake tin with greaseproof paper. Set the oven to 180°C (350°F), gas mark 4.

If you're using dates, break them up roughly with your fingers and put them into a small saucepan. Make sure that there are no stones or hard bits of stalk in with them, then add the water

162

and stir over a moderate heat until the dates are soft and mushy, mashing them with the back of a spoon as they cook. Remove from the heat and cool.

Put the dates or honey, margarine, lemon rind and eggs into a bowl, or the bowl of an electric mixer. Sift in the flour, baking powder and spice, adding the bran from the sieve at the end. Beat everything vigorously together until light, thick and fluffy-looking – this takes about 3 minutes electrically, 5 minutes by hand. Stir in the dried fruit and ground almonds. Spoon into the prepared tin, level the top and sprinkle with flaked almonds or arrange halved almonds prettily on top. Bake for 2½ hours, or until the cake is well risen, golden brown and a skewer inserted in the centre comes out clean. Cool on a wire rack; remove the paper when the cake is cold.

TO FREEZE: you can freeze this cake – follow the directions given for freezing the chocolate and honey cake – but it will keep for 2 weeks or so in a tin.

GINGERBREAD

You could use sultanas or raisins in this gingerbread instead of the chopped ginger – or you could simply leave it out – though I must say I like it best with some chunky pieces of ginger in it. It's a nice, not-too-sweet gingerbread and it will get sticky if you wrap it in foil and keep it in a tin for a week before eating.

Makes 1 20 cm (8 in) square gingerbread which cuts into 20 pieces
Calories: about 120 in each piece

125 g (4 oz) soft polyunsaturated margarine
125 g (4 oz) clear honey
125 g (4 oz) black treacle
225 g (8 oz) plain wholewheat flour
1 teaspoon bicarbonate of soda
1 teaspoon ground ginger
1 teaspoon mixed spice
150 ml (5 fl oz) milk
1 egg
50–125 g (2–4 oz) crystallized ginger, roughly chopped, or sultanas

Line a 20 cm (8 in) square tin with a piece of greaseproof paper, folded and eased into the tin so that it fits into the corners. Set the oven to 180°C (350°F), gas mark 4.

Put the margarine, honey and treacle into a medium-sized saucepan and melt over a gentle heat. Sift the flour, bicarbonate of soda and spices into a large bowl, adding the bran left behind in the sieve, too. Pour the hot melted ingredients into the flour mixture and add the milk; mix well, then beat in the egg and chopped ginger or sultanas and mix again. The mixture will be quite runny and you will have to pour it into the tin. Bake for about 45 minutes, until the gingerbread is well-risen and springs back when pressed lightly in the centre. Cool for 5 minutes or so in the tin, then transfer to a wire rack. Remove the greaseproof paper when the gingerbread is cool.

TO FREEZE: cool completely, then wrap, label and freeze. To use, unwrap and leave to defrost at room temperature.

ORANGE AND ALMOND CAKE

This comes out like a madeira cake, with a light, close texture and delicate flavour. It is very good baked in a deep tin and just finished with a sprinkling of ground almonds, or you can make it shiny by spooning honey glaze (see next section) on top and sticking some flaked almonds on to it. As with the chocolate and honey cake, you can use two sandwich tins instead of the deep one and that also works well. This way it's nice filled with the healthy butter cream in the toppings section.

Makes 1 18–20 cm (7–8 in) cake
Calories: 295 in each piece (one-tenth of cake)

175 g (6 oz) soft
  polyunsaturated margarine
175 g (6 oz) clear honey
2 large eggs
Grated rind of 1 orange and 4
  tablespoons juice
225 g (8 oz) plain wholewheat
  flour

3 teaspoons baking powder
25 g (1 oz) ground almonds –
  or you could use semolina
  or rice flour and a few
  drops of almond extract if
  you want to economize

Line the base and sides of an 18 or 20 cm (7 or 8 in) deep cake tin with greaseproof paper or if you're using two shallower tins, just put a circle of greaseproof paper in the base. Set the oven to 160°C (325°F), gas mark 3.

Put the margarine, honey, eggs, orange rind and juice into a large bowl – or the bowl of an electric mixer – and sift the flour and baking powder on top, adding also the bran which will be left in the sieve. Stir in the ground almonds, then beat everything vigorously together until smooth, thick and creamy. This takes about 3 minutes electrically, 5 minutes by hand. Spoon the mixture into the tin or tins, level the top and bake for 25–30 minutes for sandwich cakes or 1–1¼ hours for one deep cake. The cake is done when it springs back when pressed lightly in the centre with a finger. Cool on a wire rack.

TO FREEZE: as for chocolate and honey cake.

ROCK BUNS

In these rock buns date purée is used instead of sugar and we think the result is good.

Makes 12
Calories: 220 in each bun

125 g (4 oz) cooking dates, from a block
2 tablespoons water
125 g (4 oz) soft polyunsaturated margarine
225 g (8 oz) plain wholewheat flour
2 teaspoons baking powder
1 teaspoon mixed spice
125 g (4 oz) mixed dried fruit
50 g (2 oz) flaked almonds
1 egg

Break up the dates, removing any stones or hard pieces. Put the dates into a small saucepan with the water and stir over a moderate heat until the dates have reduced to a pulp. Cool.

Set the oven to 230°C (450°F), gas mark 8. Put the dates and margarine into a large bowl or the bowl of your mixer and cream together until light, then sift in the flour, baking powder and mixed spice, adding the bran left in the sieve too. Use a fork to mix the flour and spice into the fat, so that it makes a lumpy, crumbly consistency, then add the dried fruit, nuts and egg, still keeping the mixture as light and crumbly as possible.

Put rough heaps of the mixture on to a lightly greased baking sheet, pushing them together gently so that they just hold together. Bake the rock buns for 12–15 minutes. Cool on a wire rack.

TO FREEZE: cool the buns completely after baking, then wrap, label and freeze. To use, unwrap and put the buns on a wire cake rack to defrost at room temperature.

CHEESE BISCUITS

You can get round the sugar problem sometimes, I've found, by simply avoiding it and offering crisp home-made cheese biscuits instead of sweet ones. Many people in fact prefer savoury things, and these biscuits always seem to disappear fast. It's fun to experiment with different flours – they're lovely made with half wholewheat, half barley, rye or buckwheat flour, and sometimes I add some dried herbs, chopped nuts, sesame, cumin or caraway seeds, too.

Makes about 32 biscuits
Calories: 88 in each biscuit

200 g (8 oz) plain wholewheat flour, or half wholewheat and half one of the other flours
150 g (6 oz) soft polyunsaturated margarine

150 g (6 oz) grated cheese
Good pinch each of dry mustard and cayenne pepper

Set the oven to 230°C (450°F), gas mark 8. Put the flour into a bowl and mix in the margarine with a fork. Add the grated cheese, cayenne pepper and mustard. Form into a dough, roll

166

out 5 mm ($\frac{1}{4}$ in) thick, cut into 5 cm (2 in) rounds, prick each several times with a fork and bake for 15–20 minutes, until golden brown. The biscuits will get crisp as they cool. Store in an airtight tin.

TO FREEZE: cool the biscuits then put them into a rigid container and freeze. To use, spread them out on a wire cake rack to de-frost at room temperature – this will only take about 40 minutes.

SPICY CURRANT BISCUITS

The sweetness in these crisp biscuits comes from the currants, almonds and spice.

Makes 22 biscuits
Calories: 48 in each biscuit

100 g (4 oz) plain wholewheat flour
$\frac{1}{2}$ teaspoon baking powder
$\frac{1}{2}$ teaspoon allspice
50 g (2 oz) soft polyunsaturated margarine

15 g ($\frac{1}{2}$ oz) ground almonds
50 g (2 oz) currants
1 tablespoon water

Set the oven to 200°C (400°F), gas mark 6. Sift the flour, baking powder and spice into a large bowl; add the residue of bran from the sieve and the margarine, almonds and currants. Mix everything together with a fork, then stir in the water to make a dough. On a lightly-floured board roll the dough out to a thickness of about 5 mm ($\frac{1}{4}$ in). Stamp into rounds with a 5 cm (2 in) cutter, prick the top of each biscuit with a fork. Put the biscuits on floured baking sheets and bake for 10 minutes. Lift them on to wire rack to cool.

TO FREEZE: these biscuits will freeze. See instructions given for the cheese biscuits, above.

DATE SLICES

I think this is one of the nicest of the 'sugarless' biscuits, a sweet date and vanilla purée sandwiched between two layers of light wholewheat and oat pastry.

Makes 18
Calories: 130 in each slice

225 g (8 oz) cooking dates, from a block
4 tablespoons water
1 teaspoon extract of vanilla
1 tablespoon honey

125 g (4 oz) wholewheat flour
125 g (4 oz) porridge oats
125 g (4 oz) soft polyunsaturated margarine

Break up the dates, removing any stones and hard pieces. Put the dates into a saucepan with the water and cook gently to a purée. Cool; add the vanilla.

Set the oven to 200°C (400°F), gas mark 6. Lightly grease an 18 cm (7 in) square tin. Put the flour and oats into a large bowl and use a fork to blend in the margarine and honey. Mix to a dough, then press half of this into the prepared tin. Spread with the date mixture, top with the rest of the flour and oat mixture. Press down very firmly. Bake for 25–30 minutes. Cool in the tin, then cut into sections with a sharp knife and ease the pieces out of the tin with a palette knife.

TO FREEZE: open-freeze the slices, store in a polythene bag. Put them on a wire rack to defrost.

JAM AND ALMOND FINGERS

The 'jam' in these is one of the beautiful new sugarless ones now available from health shops. My favourites are the pear and apple, a lovely deep red colour with a very fruity flavour, and the apricot and damson ones, which are lower in calories. In this recipe the jam is melted over a light, crisp wholewheat shortcrust base, to make a shiny glaze, which is topped with crunchy flaked almonds. It's good with other nuts, too: chopped roasted hazel nuts and also chopped Brazils.

Makes 20
Calories: 100 in each slice if made with pear and apple jam; 85 with apricot or damson.

200 g (6 oz) plain wholewheat
   flour
100 g (3 oz) soft
   polyunsaturated margarine
4 teaspoons cold water

225 g (8 oz) sugarless jam –
   preferably pear and apple,
   apricot or damson
25 g (1 oz) flaked almonds

Set the oven to 200°C (400°F), gas mark 6. Put the flour into a large bowl and use a fork to blend in the margarine. Add the water and mix to a dough. On a lightly-floured board roll out the dough to fit a 30 × 20 (12 × 8) Swiss roll tin. The easiest way to transfer the crumbly wholewheat pastry is to tip it straight from the board to the tin. Prick the base and bake the pastry for 15–20 minutes, until golden and crisp. Put the jam into a medium-sized saucepan and melt over a fairly gentle heat, then pour it evenly over the pastry and sprinkle with the almonds. Leave to cool. The pastry will crisp and the glaze will set. The pear and apple jam sets better than the others, which may need to go in the fridge to become really firm. Cut into slices.

TO FREEZE: freeze as for the date slices, above.

JAM TARTS

You can make nice little jam tarts using wholewheat pastry and the sugarless jam. The quantity of pastry given above makes about 18 Either make the tartlet cases first, then melt the jam and pour into the tartlets, as for the jam and almond slice above, or put about a teaspoonful of jam into each tart before baking, then bake for about 15 minutes.

Calories: 100 in each tart with pear and apple jam; 85 with apricot

TO FREEZE: as for date slice.

Icings, Fillings, Creams and Toppings

If cakes and biscuits leave quite a lot to be desired from the health point of view, most icings and toppings are even worse, being mainly composed of fat or sugar or both.

However, once you begin to think of healthy low-fat, low-sugar alternatives, it's surprising how many you find. At the simplest level, there are some delicious sugarless jams on the market now and you can use these instead of ordinary jam to sandwich cakes together: the pear and apple jam (which is red, with a very fruity flavour) is particularly good, and one of the sharp-tasting sugarless marmalades is nice in a lemon or orange cake.

You can also use the date filling in the drinks, sweets and preserves section in the same way, and in the summer, if you're making a cake that will be eaten up fairly quickly, soft fruit mashed with a little honey makes a lovely filling.

These fruity fillings and jams are good in sandwich cakes either on their own or with a layer of one of the rich-tasting creams from this section too. Or you can use the creams on their own – the 'healthy' butter icing is really a replacement for conventional butter icing. However nothing quite takes the place of a sparkling white royal icing and you may like to use this for special occasions such as Christmas or a wedding. The funny thing is, though, that once you begin to think about healthy cooking it becomes quite distasteful even to work with refined sugar products.

So I offer these ideas instead. You can make an excellent version of almond paste using honey and I don't think many people could tell the difference between this and the real thing, so that isn't a problem. Instead of icing you can use the honey frosting, which turns out light and sweet and almost as white as royal icing and is, I think, a good replacement for both royal icing and glacé icing, although it only keeps for a few days.

Of course you can do away with almond paste and icing altogether and make the cake shine with honey glaze and perhaps stick some pieces of glace fruit and nuts on top for a once-a-year

Christmas treat. Another quick finish for everyday is to sprinkle the top of cakes, pies and tarts with a little ground almond.

The creams in this section also make very good toppings for fruit salads and puddings; I particularly like the slightly sharp-tasting low-fat cheese ones which I think taste rather like the French *crème fraîche*. I have also given recipes for some healthy pouring creams and for an almond custard.

ALMOND CUSTARD

Arrowroot is an acceptable healthy alternative to cornflour and makes a lovely low-fat almond custard.

Serves 4
Calories: 60 in each serving

1 tablespoon arrowroot
1 tablespoon ground almonds
300 ml (10 fl oz) skimmed
  milk

2 teaspoons honey
A few drops of almond
  extract

Put all ingredients into the liquidizer and blend. Pour into a saucepan and stir over a gentle heat until thickened.

TO FREEZE: freeze in a rigid container; to use, thaw at room temperature then heat gently, stirring.

ALMOND PASTE

Although this doesn't contain sugar, it tastes like conventional almond paste and can be used similarly.

Makes 350 g (12 oz)
Calories: about 130 for 28 g (1 oz)

50 g (2 oz) unsalted
  polyunsaturated margarine
1 tablespoon thick honey
2 teaspoons lemon juice

425 g (4 oz) rice flour
425 g (4 oz) ground almonds
A few drops of almond
  extract

Mix all the ingredients together, flavouring with a little almond extract. Handle the mixture lightly to avoid the almonds becoming oily.

TO FREEZE: wrap in polythene then freeze.

LOW-FAT BUTTERCREAM

This is a sort of healthy butter icing; there's no sugar in it and it's lower in fat than conventional butter creams.

Makes about 275 g (10 oz)
Calories: about 54 in 28 g (1 oz)

2 level teaspoons arrowroot
150 ml ($\frac{1}{4}$ pint) skimmed milk
40 g ($1\frac{1}{2}$ oz) unsalted
  polyunsaturated margarine

1 tablespoon honey
$\frac{1}{2}$ teaspoon extract of vanilla

Put the arrowroot into a small saucepan and blend to a paste with the milk. Heat gently, stirring all the time, until thickened. Remove from the heat and leave to get completely cold. Cream together the margarine, honey and vanilla, then add the arrowroot mixture a little at a time, beating well to make a light, fluffy mixture.

TO FREEZE: freeze in a small rigid container. Thaw at room temperature; beat before using.

HONEY FROSTING

You make this like an American frosting except that you use

172

honey instead of sugar. It sets to a mallowy texture and looks like a conventional icing. You can use it to fill and ice cakes or as a topping for buns. It makes a very good peaky snowy topping for a Christmas cake but only keeps for a few days.

Makes enough to cover a 20 cm (8 in) cake
Calories: 730 in all; about 75 in 28 g (1 oz)

1 large egg white
Pinch of cream of tartar

225 g (8 oz) clear honey

This is easiest if you've got an electric whisk, though it can be done by hand. Put the egg white and cream of tartar into a bowl, or the bowl of your electric mixer, and whisk until stiff. Heat the honey in a small saucepan until a little of it dropped into cold water will form a soft ball. This isn't nearly as complicated as it sounds – just let the honey bubble away for about 3 or 4 minutes and you're there. If you've got a sugar thermometer it should be 115°C (240°F). Pour the hot honey on to the egg white, whisking as you do so. Continue to whisk until the mixture is very light and thick and fluffy – it will also get whiter. This takes about 5 minutes electrically, 10 or 15 minutes by hand. Spread over the cake immediately and leave to set.

TO FREEZE: unsuitable.

HONEY GLAZE

If you boil honey for a few minutes it will set to a clear glaze and this makes an attractive topping for some cakes. You can leave the glaze as it is or sprinkle some chopped or flaked nuts over it.

Cover the top of a 20 cm (8 in) round cake
Calories: 340 in all; 85 in 28 g (1 oz) (without the nuts)

125 g (4 oz) clear honey
A few nuts to decorate,
    optional

Have the cake ready for the topping before you start, because this glaze hardens quickly. Put the honey into a small saucepan and let it bubble over a moderate heat for 3–4 minutes, being careful that the honey does not burn, until a little dropped into a saucer of cold water forms a hard ball. Remove the saucepan from the stove and pour the glaze quickly over the top of the cake. Scatter a few nuts on top if you wish.

TO FREEZE: unsuitable.

DOUBLE CREAM (UNSATURATED)

This cream is very much like real double cream, except there's no saturated fat in it, so it's better for you. You really do need an unsalted polyunsaturated margarine to make it and you should be able to get this at a health shop. I've come across a brand called Vitaquell – it's beautiful with a delicate flavour, and pale colour. If you don't eat dairy produce, you could also make this using a non-dairy milk.

Makes 150 ml (5 fl oz)
Calories: 125 calories in a tablespoonful

150 g (5 oz) unsalted
  polyunsaturated margarine
150 ml (5 fl oz) skimmed
  milk

2 teaspoons clear honey
½ teaspoon vanilla extract

Cut the margarine into small pieces and put into a small saucepan with the milk. Heat gently until the margarine has melted. Pour the milk mixture into the liquidizer and blend for 1 minute, until smooth. Pour into a small bowl and chill in the fridge for at least 2–3 hours. Add the honey and vanilla then whisk vigorously – don't worry if at first it looks as though it's going to curdle; just keep whisking and it will become thick, just like ordinary whipped cream. You can also make a pouring version of this, like single cream, by increasing the milk to 300 ml (10 fl oz).

TO FREEZE: unsuitable.

POURING CREAM, UNSATURATED

This is another pouring cream, again unsaturated, which my daughters love.

Makes just under 150 ml ($\frac{1}{4}$ pint)
Calories: 58 in 1 level tablespoonful

50 g (2 oz) unsalted
  polyunsaturated margarine
3 rounded tablespoons
  skimmed milk granules

75 ml (3 fl oz) water

Melt the margarine over a gentle heat. Put the skimmed milk powder, water and melted margarine into the liquidizer and blend to a smooth cream. Pour into a small jug and chill thoroughly – it will thicken up a little. Stir, then serve. Can be sweetened slightly with a very little clear honey if liked.

TO FREEZE: unsuitable.

POURING CREAM (LOW-FAT)

This is a slightly sweetened cream which has the consistency of single cream. It's good with fruit salads.

Makes about 100 ml (4 fl oz)
Calories: 12 in a tablespoonful

50 g (2 oz) fromage blanc
6 tablespoons liquid skimmed
  milk

Clear honey to taste
  ($\frac{1}{4}$–1 teaspoon)

Put the fromage blanc into a small bowl and add the milk and a little honey as desired; beat until smooth and creamy. Chill; stir before serving.

TO FREEZE: unsuitable.

THICK CREAM FILLING OR TOPPING

This looks like whipped cream and you can even pipe with it if you wish. It makes an excellent topping for fruit salads and other puddings and can replace double cream in cakes. I like the sharp-tasting plain version, without either the honey or vanilla, but the rest of the family prefer it with the honey and vanilla.

Makes about 150 ml (5 fl oz)
Calories: 30–50 in a tablespoonful, depending on amount of honey used

125 g (4 oz) fromage blanc
2 tablespoons natural yoghurt
1–2 teaspoons clear honey,
   optional

$\frac{1}{2}$–1 teaspoon extract of
vanilla, optional

Put the fromage blanc into a bowl and add the other ingredients. Beat well until light and creamy and the consistency of whipped double cream.

TO FREEZE: unsuitable.

Breads and Scones

If you make your own bread you know what's in it, for although wholewheat flour cannot contain additives, wholewheat bread can. That is not to say that it always does: some bakers and many health shops sell beautiful additive-free wholewheat bread, but you need to check and unless you're sure of your supplier you might feel that you'd prefer to make most of your bread yourself.

Breadmaking isn't the long and difficult business many people suppose and both the recipes I've given are simple, particularly the quick easy loaf which really does take very little time to make.

Once you get into the way of breadmaking it is fun to vary the basic recipes by using different flours – rye and barley flour are very pleasant additions, but need to be used with wheat flour as they do not contain much gluten and so don't rise well on their own. A half and half mixture or two-thirds wheat flour to one-third rye or barley are good proportions.

You can also replace a little of the wheat flour with some bran or wheatgerm and use honey or black treacle instead of sugar to sweeten and flavour the loaf. Dried fruit and chopped nuts can be added and so can cumin or caraway seeds, cinnamon or cardamom. Or you can make a lovely savoury loaf by adding some chopped onion or crushed garlic and fragrant herbs such as rosemary, thyme and dill.

And of course you can finish the loaf with all kinds of different toppings: kibbled wheat is always attractive, but chopped nuts or poppy, sesame, aniseed, cumin and caraway seeds are pleasant for a change, and grated cheese is good on top of a savoury loaf.

QUICK EASY BREAD

If you've never made bread before, this is the one to start with.

It doesn't need kneading and it really is as quick as making a simple cake. The texture is a little different from ordinary bread, being moister, which means that the bread keeps well and the flavour is very good. It is sometimes called the 'Grant loaf', after its inventor, Doris Grant, one of the pioneers of healthy eating. This quantity makes two 450 g (1 lb) loaves. You can bake it all in one 900 g (2 lb) loaf tin, but I think it comes out better in two smaller tins. You do need to use all wholewheat flour, by the way, for this particular recipe to work.

Makes 2 450 g (1 lb) loaves
Calories: 60 in 28 g (1 oz)

425 ml (¾ pint) hand-hot
  water
2 teaspoons sugar
1 tablespoon dried yeast

500 g (1 lb 2 oz) wholewheat
  flour
1½ teaspoons salt
Kibbled wheat for topping

Put the water into a jug or bowl and stir in the sugar and yeast. Leave on one side for 10 minutes – it will froth up like a glass of beer. Meanwhile thoroughly grease two 450 g (1 lb) loaf tins or one 900 g (2 lb) tin – I think butter is the best fat to use for this as it does seem to prevent the loaves from sticking to the tins.

Put the flour and salt into a large bowl, or the bowl of your electric mixer. Pour in the frothy yeast mixture and mix well to a smooth but sticky dough – it won't be firm enough to knead. Spoon the dough into the tins or tin – it should come halfway up the sides. Sprinkle with some kibbled wheat, pressing it down lightly with the back of a spoon. Cover the bread lightly with a piece of polythene and leave it to rise. It should come to within 1 cm (½ in) of the top of the tin and I find this takes 30 minutes at room temperature. (The bread will rise a bit more when it gets into the oven.)

Set the oven to 200°C (400°F), gas mark 6 after the bread has been rising for 15 minutes. Bake the bread for 30 minutes for small loaves, 40 minutes for large. Turn out the bread and cool on a wire rack.

If you like this bread you might like to make a larger batch. Use a whole 1·5 kg (3 lb 5 oz) and treble all the ingredients except the yeast: 1·3 litres (2¼ pints) water, 2 level tablespoons sugar, a slightly rounded tablespoon of salt and 2 tablespoons (or one sachet) of dried yeast. These quantities make 6 small or 3 large loaves.

TO FREEZE: this bread freezes very well. Just pop the loaves into polythene bags and freeze. To use, remove polythene and stand the loaves on a rack to thaw.

WHOLEWHEAT BREAD

This is the other bread recipe which I use regularly. It takes a little longer than the previous one because the bread is kneaded in the usual way and I like to let it rise twice, which makes for a lovely light loaf. Although the bread-making process spreads over two or three hours, during most of that time the bread is just sitting on one side proving or rising, so it really isn't as daunting as it seems.

Makes 5 450 g (1 lb) loaves
Calories: about 63 in 28 g (1 oz)

300 ml (11 fl oz) hand-hot
  water
2 tablespoons clear honey,
  sugar or treacle
2 level tablespoons (or 1
  sachet) dried yeast
1·5 kg (3 lb 5 oz) wholewheat
  flour

4 teaspoons salt
50 g (2 oz) polyunsaturated
  margarine
600 ml (21 fl oz) hand-hot
  water
Kibbled wheat

Put the 300 ml (11 fl oz) water into a jug or bowl and stir in ½ teaspoon of honey, sugar or treacle and the dried yeast. Mix with a fork, then leave on one side for 10 minutes for the yeast to start working and froth up like a glass of beer.

Meanwhile grease five 450 g (1 lb) loaf tins with butter and leave on one side. Put the flour into a large bowl – or, if you have an electric mixer with dough hooks, the bowl of your mixer – together with the remaining honey, sugar or treacle, the salt and the margarine. Mix everything together lightly, then pour in the frothy yeast mixture and the 600 ml (21 fl oz) water. Work the yeast and water into the flour with your hands until a dough is formed. Knead this dough for 5 minutes electrically, or 10 minutes by hand. If you're kneading by hand it's easiest to turn the dough out on to a clean working surface and knead it on that. It's a very satisfying experience to feel the rough, sticky lump of dough become smooth and pliable as you work it.

Put the kneaded dough back into the large bowl and cover with a piece of oiled polythene – one of those big supermarket carrier bags is good and will sit completely over the bowl. Leave the dough until doubled in size. This takes exactly 1 hour in my kitchen, which is fairly warm, but may take longer in a cooler place: that doesn't matter and you will soon get to know the right timing for the temperature in your kitchen. You can even leave the dough to rise overnight in the fridge if that is more convenient for you.

When the dough has risen, punch your fist into it and then knead it for another 1–2 minutes. Divide the dough into five equal-sized pieces. I find the easiest way to do this is to weigh them; they should each be 500 g (1 lb 2 oz). Form the dough into loaves, roll them in kibbled wheat and put them into the prepared tins. Cover the tins again with polythene and leave to rise – this time it will only take about 30 minutes. Set the oven to 230°C (450° F), gas mark 8.

When the dough is just level with the top of the tins at the sides and higher in the centre put it into the oven. (Don't let it get higher than this because if the bread has over-risen it will flop when it gets into the oven.) Bake the bread for 10 minutes, then reduce the oven temperature to 200°C (400° F), gas mark 6 and bake for a further 25 minutes. Turn the loaves out of their tins and tap them on the base with your knuckles. They should sound hollow – if they don't, put them back in the oven for a few minutes. Cool the loaves on a wire rack.

TO FREEZE: as for quick, easy bread.

WHOLEWHEAT ROLLS

These are useful for serving with all kinds of different meals, and you can make them from some of the bread dough. After the dough has risen once, take about half or one-third of it and mix in an egg and 25 g (1 oz) extra margarine. You might need just

180

a little more flour too, but the mixture can be quite soft. Form into 18 rolls, press a little kibbled wheat into the top of each and place on a lightly greased and floured baking sheet, with enough space between each to allow for spreading. They will only take about 20 minutes to rise and about 15–20 to cook, as above.

Calories: 175 per roll

TO FREEZE: as for quick, easy bread.

WHOLEWHEAT SCONES

These are a great standby because they're so quick to make. Turn on the oven, mix up the ingredients and you can be eating hot fresh scones less than 30 minutes later! You can even have a healthy version of a 'cream tea' if you serve the warm scones with one of the sugarless jams and lashings of creamy low-fat quark – a very good combination.

Makes 12
Calories: 120 in each scone

225 g (8 oz) plain wholewheat
  flour
4 teaspoons baking powder

50 g (2 oz) soft
  polyunsaturated margarine
2 tablespoons honey
8 tablespoons milk

Set the oven to 220 C (425 F), gas mark 7. Sift the flour and baking powder into a large bowl, adding also the residue of bran from the sieve. Mix in the margarine and honey with a fork, then add the milk to make a soft dough. Press the dough out to a thickness of 1 cm ($\frac{1}{2}$ in) on a floured board, then stamp into 5 cm (2 in) rounds with a pastry cutter. Place the scones on a lightly-floured baking sheet and bake for 10 minutes, until set and well-risen. Cool on a wire rack.

TO FREEZE: cook then open-freeze; pack and label. To use, put the scones on a wire rack and thaw at room temperature. Warm in the oven before using.

CHEESE SCONES

These are lovely with salads and something you can produce
quickly to serve with a soup to make it into more of a meal. The
mixture is the same as above, except that instead of the honey you
use 12 tablespoons (180 ml [6 fl oz]) milk and 75–100 g (3–4 oz)
finely grated cheese. A teaspoonful of mustard is nice added to this
mixture, and so are a few sesame seeds. The scones can also be
brushed over with some beaten egg and sprinkled with cracked
wheat, sesame seeds, caraway, cumin, mustard or poppy seeds for
an interesting finish.

Calories: about 140 each

TO FREEZE: as above.

Drinks, Sweets and Preserves

ALMOND PASTE SWEETS

The almond paste on page 171 makes good sweets. Colour the almond paste with vegetable colourings if you like and roll it into little fruits or whatever shapes you fancy. If you have young children they will have plenty of ideas but will probably eat most of it. It's good at Christmas as a filling for shiny dates, instead of the stone, or to stick two walnut halves together with or as a thin coating for Brazil nuts which can then be rolled lightly in cocoa or carob powder.

Calories: about 130 for 28 g

TO FREEZE: Open-freeze, pack. To use, spread out on a wire rack or plate and thaw.

NUT, RAISIN AND DATE 'FUDGE'

This isn't quite like real fudge, but it's not a bad approximation, especially when you consider that it doesn't contain any added sugar or fat. You need powdered skimmed milk from health shops, not the ordinary granules.

Makes 24 pieces
Calories: 48 a piece, without rum

125 g (4 oz) cooking dates
   from a block
50 ml (2 fl oz) water
1 tablespoon carob or cocoa
   powder
1–2 teaspoons vanilla extract
6 tablespoons skimmed milk
   powder

4 tablespoons ground
   almonds
4 tablespoons chopped mixed
   nuts
50 g (2 oz) raisins
1–2 teaspoons rum – optional

Cut the dates into pieces and put them into a small saucepan
with the water. Heat gently, stirring often, until dates have
softened to a thick purée. Remove from heat and mix in the
remaining ingredients, beating well – the mixture will be quite
stiff. Spread into a lightly oiled Swiss roll tin, making the mixture
about 1 cm ($\frac{1}{2}$ in) deep (it won't fill the whole tin). Smooth top
and leave on one side for at least 2 hours to firm up. Cut into
squares to serve.

TO FREEZE: open-freeze, pack. Thaw at room temperature.

NUTTY GINGER CLUSTERS

These are my favourites, shiny little heaps of chopped nuts and
ginger.

Makes 8
Calories: 80 in each

1 tablespoon clear honey
75 g (3 oz) chopped nuts

2 pieces of preserved ginger,
   finely chopped, about 1$\frac{1}{2}$ oz

Put the honey into a small saucepan and heat gently for 3–4
minutes, until a little forms a hard ball when dropped into a saucer
of cold water. Stir frequently and be careful not to let it burn.
Remove from the heat, add the other ingredients. Put little heaps
of the mixture into tiny paper cases or on to waxed paper and
leave to set.

TO FREEZE: open-freeze then pack. Thaw at room temperature.

ICED LOLLIES

Lolly moulds are widely available and I find you can make lovely professional-looking lollies with them. You simply push a stick – they're supplied with the moulds, and you can buy more separately – into the mould, pour in some fruit juice or fruit yoghurt and leave in the freezing part of the fridge or in the freezer until firm. They're quite easy to get out of the moulds and are an excellent healthy alternative to ordinary lollies. The children love both making and eating them.

Calories: about 30 for a pineapple lolly; 20 for orange and 40 for fruit yoghurt

---

CHUTNEY

This is an easy chutney that you don't have to cook and all the sweetening comes from the dried fruit – this natural sugar, together with the vinegar, means that the chutney keeps perfectly.

Makes just under 2 kg (about 4 lbs)
Calories: about 20 for 1 level tablespoonful

450 g (1 lb) cooking dates
   from a block
550 ml (1 pint) vinegar
450 g (1 lb) cooking apples,
   peeled and grated
450 g (1 lb) onions, peeled
   and finely chopped

1 teaspoon salt
½ teaspoon each cayenne
   pepper, allspice and ground
   ginger

Break up the dates and remove any stones and pieces of stem. Put the dates into a bowl with the vinegar and leave until softened, then stir in all the other ingredients. Leave mixture to stand for 24 hours, stirring from time to time, then put into clean bottles.

You can add other ingredients to this basic mixture; I like it with a couple of tablespoons of mustard seeds in it – they give a crunchy texture.

DATE SPREAD

This spread can be used in place of jam on bread or as a filling for cakes. It can be flavoured in different ways, and you can even make a chocolate version by stirring in some cocoa or carob powder. I've just given a small quantity as it needs to be kept in the fridge and used up fairly quickly.

Makes 450 g (1 lb)
Calories: about 30 for a tablespoonful

225 g (8 oz) cooking dates
   from a block
300 ml (10 fl oz) water
A little lemon juice

Break up the dates, removing any stones and pieces of stem. Put the dates into a saucepan with the water and cook gently until soft. Sharpen with a little lemon juice to taste. Keep in a jar in the fridge.

NON-SUGAR MARMALADE

This is quite like real marmalade but keep it in the fridge as it hasn't got the sugar to preserve it.

Makes 225 g (8 oz)
Calories: about 25 in a tablespoonful

275 ml ($\frac{1}{2}$ pint) orange juice
4 teaspoons honey
1 teaspoon agar agar – from
   health shops

Pared rind of 2 large oranges
   and 1 lemon

Put the orange juice and honey into a saucepan and bring to the boil. Gradually sprinkle in the agar agar, mixing or whisking well as you do so. When it has all been incorporated, let the mixture bubble for 1 minute. Remove from the heat, stir in the orange and lemon rind. Cool, then pour into a clean jar.

PINEAPPLE JAM

This is another preserve which has to be kept in the fridge but it makes a pleasant spread or cake filling.

Makes just under 225 g (8 oz)
Calories: about 20 in a tablespoonful

225 g (8 oz) can pineapple   2 teaspoons arrowroot
  rings in their own juice

Liquidize the pineapple with the arrowroot. Pour into a saucepan and heat, stirring, until the mixture thickens and looks translucent. Cool and bottle.

PINEAPPLE MINCEMEAT

I suddenly thought, when I was about to make mincemeat, why add sugar and fat? You don't need the sugar because there is enough in the dried fruit and that, together with the brandy, will preserve the mincemeat. The traditional suet isn't necessary, either, and makes mince pies fattier than they need be. You can do away with both and make fresh-tasting, delicious mincemeat.

Makes about 2 kg (4 lb)
Calories: about 60 in 28 g (1 oz)

350 g (12 oz) cooking dates
from a block
150 ml (5 fl oz) brandy
225 g (8 oz) each of currants,
sultanas and chopped
stoned raisins
75 g (3 oz) candied peel,
chopped
Grated rind of 1 lemon
Grated rind and juice of
1 orange

50 g (2 oz) blanched almonds,
chopped
1 teaspoon mixed spice
350 g (12 oz) cooking apples,
peeled and grated
350 g (12 oz) pineapple
canned in juice, drained
and chopped

Put everything into a bowl and mix well together. Spoon into clean, sterilized jars, only three-quarters filling the jars and pressing down the mincemeat well with a spoon to remove as much air as possible. Press a piece of greaseproof paper down on top of the mincemeat before you put the lid on the jar. Label and store. If you store this mincemeat in your kitchen, you may find it starts to ferment if the kitchen is warm. Don't worry if this happens; the space in the jar allows for this and when the mixture has stopped fizzing you can use the mincemeat in one of the jars to fill the others to the top. The mincemeat will be perfectly all right and taste delicious.

MILK SHAKE

If you keep a bottle of skimmed milk and some fruit yoghurt in the fridge you can make this very quickly. The children like it served in a tall glass with a straw.

Makes 1 glassful
Calories: 115

200 ml (7 fl oz) chilled
skimmed milk
2 tablespoons fruit yoghurt,

preferably one without
artificial colouring and
flavouring

Put the skimmed milk and yoghurt into the liquidizer and blend until well mixed and frothy. Serve at once.

FORTIFIED MILK

This a good 'liquid lunch' for those days when you're too busy to think about eating. It's lovely either hot or cold and is surprisingly sustaining. It's even better if you can put your feet up for ten minutes while you drink it.

Makes 1 glassful
Calories: 160

200 ml (7 fl oz) skimmed   2 tablespoons skimmed milk
   milk, hot or chilled   powder or granules

Blend the milk and milk powder in the liquidizer until frothy. Pour into a glass and serve at once. You can add various flavourings such as cinnamon, ginger, allspice or nutmeg, cocoa or carob powder or vanilla extract, but it's good as it is, creamy yet light.

FRUIT CUP WITH VERMOUTH

A friend of mine serves this lovely fruit cup as an aperitif; it's beautifully refreshing. All you do is mix together equal quantities of apple juice, orange juice and white vermouth (Chambéry is best), all well chilled. Then add a few sprigs of fresh mint and a few slices of orange, lemon and/or cucumber, as available. You can use a still apple juice or a sparkling one if you want some bubbles.

Calories: 72 for 125 ml (4 fl oz)

APPLE JUICE WITH MINT

This is just two-thirds still apple juice and one-third soda or Perrier water with some chopped mint and an ice cube. It's very refreshing on a hot day.

Calories: 60 for a 300 ml ($\frac{1}{2}$ pint) glassful

PINEAPPLE JUICE WITH PERRIER WATER

Pineapple juice on its own is rather sweet, but a half and half mixture of pineapple juice and Perrier water (or soda water) makes a pleasant drink. Some cubes of ice are nice in it, and a slice of lemon.

Calories: about 60 for a 300 ml ($\frac{1}{2}$ pint) glassful

Calorie Counter

Calories per 28 g (1 oz) (unless otherwise stated)

Food	calories
Beans, baked	26
broad, boiled	12
butter, cooked	26
butter, uncooked	76
chick peas, cooked	26
chick peas, uncooked	78
French, boiled	2
haricots, cooked	25
haricots, dried	73
kidney, cooked	25
kidney, dried	73
lentils, cooked	27
lentils, uncooked	84
runner, boiled	2
Beverages	
carob	100
cocoa	128
coffee	0
tea	0
Biscuits	
crispbread, one	30
digestive, one	60
chocolate	150–160
shortbread finger, one	90

Food	calories
Bran	62
1 tablespoon	16
Bread, wholewheat	63
Cakes	
Fruit cake	100–115
Victoria sponge	115
Fatless sponge	90
Carob powder	100
Cereals, breakfast	
All Bran	88
Bran	62
Grapenuts	102
Muesli base	105
Oats, rolled	110
Puffed wheat	100
Shredded wheat	100
Weetabix	100
Wheatgerm	105
Cereals, whole grain	
barley	100
buckwheat	98
oats	110
rice, brown	102
rye	105
wheat	94
Cheese	
brie	75
camembert	85
cheshire	90
cottage	30
curd	40
cream	130
edam	85

Food	calories
fromage blanc	30
other hard cheeses	100–120
parmesan	110
parmesan, 1 tablespoonful	30
quark	42
Chutney	20–40
mango, 1 tablespoonful	35
Cream	
double	131
single	62
soured	60
Cocoa powder	128
Coffee	0
Crispbread, 1 average	30
Drinks, soft	
ginger ale, 125 ml (4 fl oz)	40
lemonade, 125 ml (4 fl oz)	30
bitter lemon, 125 ml (4 fl oz)	40
Eggs, 1 standard	80
white only	11
Fats and oils	
butter	225
margarine	225
vegetable oil	250
vegetable oil, 1 tablespoon	125
vegetable oil, 1 teaspoonful	42
Fish (without bone etc.)	
anchovies	50
cod, coley	23

Food	Calories
Fish – *cont.*	
crab	35
haddock	28
halibut	37
herring, fresh	37
kipper	51
oysters	14
pilchards	60
plaice	26
prawns	30
salmon, fresh	57
canned	39
sardines, canned	84
sole	24
trout	38
tuna, fresh	37
canned	72
whiting	27
Flours	
arrowroot	101
barley	100
buckwheat	98
cornflour	100
oatmeal	110
rice	102
rye	105
wholewheat	94
Fruit, dried	
apple rings	71
apricots	54
currants	72
dates, stoned	74
figs	61
peaches	61
prunes	38
raisins	75
sultanas	72

Food	calories
Fruit, fresh	
apples, one, 100 g (4 oz)	40
apricots	8
avocado pear, ½ medium	320
banana, one medium	80
blackberries	8
cherries, fresh	11
glace, one	10
currants	8
damsons	11
dates, unstoned	70
gooseberries, ripe	10
grapefruit, 1 medium half	15
grapes	18
greengages	13
kiwi fruit	10
lemon, whole	4
lychees, flesh only	20
mandarins, fresh, one medium	20
mango, fresh	15
melon, cantaloup, honeydew, ogen	
water, flesh only	7
nectarines	14
oranges, fresh	10
peaches, fresh, 1 medium	35
pears, fresh, 1 medium	50
pineapple, fresh	13
canned in own juice	13
plums, dessert, fresh, 1 medium	15
raspberries, fresh	7
rhubarb, 1 stick	5
strawberries, fresh	7
tangerines, fresh, 1 medium	20

Fruit juice, see Juices

Ginger, preserved in syrup 80

Grains, see cereals, whole grain

Food	calories
Honey, average	85
1 teaspoon	30
Ice Cream	56
Jam	
apricot and others similar (sugarless)	37
pear and apple	70
marmalade	75
1 teaspoonful	25
Juices, unsweetened	
apple, 125 ml (4 fl oz)	40
grape, 125 ml (4 fl oz)	76
grapefruit, 125 ml (4 fl oz)	44
lemon, 1 tablespoon	0
orange, 125 ml (4 fl oz)	44
pineapple, 125 ml (4 fl oz)	60
tomato, 150 (5 fl oz)	30
Liqueurs, 25 ml (1 fl oz), average	100
Marmalade	75
1 teaspoonful	25
sugarless	37
Meat	
bacon, grilled	120
beef, average fat and lean	49
chicken, on bone, baked	30
ham, lean, boiled	63
kidney, all kinds, raw	25
lamb, average fat and lean	80
liver, average	40
pate, liver	80
pheasant, on bone	30
pork, average fat and lean	120
rabbit, on bone	26
sausage, pork, grilled, 1 medium	115
tongue, ox	85
turkey, on bone	34

Food	calories
Milk	
powdered skim	90
1 level tablespoonful	25
skimmed, liquid	10
soya, liquid	10
whole	19
Nuts, shelled	
almonds, whole, flaked, ground	170
ground, 1 tablespoon	40
Brazil	183
cashew	178
chestnuts, fresh	49
coconut, fresh	104
desiccated, unsweetened	178
hazel	108
peanuts	171
peanut butter	180
pistachio	166
walnuts	151
Nutmeats	
nutbrawn, Granose	37
nuttolene, Granose	87
meatless steaks, Granose	37
rissol-nut, Granose (dry)	129
sausalatas	36
Pasta, wholewheat, cooked	35
uncooked	105
Peanut butter	180
1 tablespoonful	90
Pickled gherkins	5
Preserves, jam, marmalade etc.	75
1 teaspoonful	25
apricot and others similar (sugarless)	37
pear and apple	70

Food	calories

Salad dressings
Dietade, Appleford	1
fat-free French dressing,	
1½ tablespoons (28 g [1 oz])	5
mayonnaise, 1 tablespoon (28 g [1 oz])	200
salad cream, 1 tablespoon	55

Sauces and flavourings
horseradish sauce, 1 tablespoon	15
mango chutney, 1 tablespoon	35
mint sauce, 1 tablespoon (28 g [1 oz])	40
mustard, made, 1 tablespoon	30
mustard, powder, 1 teaspoon	20
soy sauce, 1 tablespoon	5
tomato ketchup, 1 tablespoon (28 g [1 oz])	35
tomato paste, 1 tablespoon	10
yeast extract	2

Seeds
pumpkin	155
sesame	160
sesame cream (tahini)	160
sunflower	170

Sherry, 25 ml (1 fl oz), dry	30
medium	35
cream	40

Spirits, gin, rum, vodka, whisky,	
25 ml (1 fl oz)	60

Sweeteners
black treacle	75
honey, average	82–90
jam or marmalade, 1 teaspoon	25
molasses	70
sugar, all types	112
1 teaspoon	15

Food	calories
Vegetables	
artichoke	
cooked globe, 225 g (8 oz)	15
Jerusalem	5
asparagus, cooked	5
aubergines	4
beans, broad	12
French and runner	4
beansprouts	8
beetroot	13
broccoli	4
brussels sprouts	10
cabbage	6
carrots	6
cauliflower	7
celery	3
cucumber	3
garlic, a clove	2
greens	3
leeks	9
lettuce	3
marrow or courgettes	3
mushrooms	2
mustard and cress	3
olive, one	7
onions	6
parsley	6
parsnips	14
peas	18
peppers	9
potatoes	24
radish	4
spinach	7
spring onions	10
swedes	6
sweetcorn, frozen or canned	20
whole cob, medium	85
tomato	4
turnip	5

Food	calories
watercress	4
Wheatgerm	105
1 tablespoonful	25
Wines	
dry white 125 ml (4 fl oz)	75
sparkling white 125 ml (4 fl oz)	90
sweet white 125 ml (4 fl oz)	100
dry red, rosé 125 ml (4 fl oz)	80
sweet red 125 ml (4 fl oz)	95
ginger wine 125 ml (4 fl oz)	230
port 25 ml (1 fl oz)	45
sherry, dry, small glass	55
sherry, sweet, small glass	60
vermouth, sweet, small glass	60
Yoghurt (1 tbs, 28 g [1 oz])	
low-fat, natural	15
fruit flavoured	22
whole milk, natural	20

Index

201

203